TRUCKS IN CAMERA
SCAMMELL

TRUCKS IN CAMERA
SCAMMELL

John Reed

LONDON

IAN ALLAN LTD

Photo Credits

Unless otherwise credited all photographs are from the Ian Allan Library.

ARC Ltd 59 (both), 60 (both); Boughton Group 90 (B); Chubb Ltd 27 (T), 93 (both); Crane Fruehauf Trailers 90 (T); Dyson Trailers 86 (T); English China Clays Ltd 50 (B), 61 (T), 62 (both); Ford & Slater Ltd 57 (both); Gloster Saro 92 (B); Imperial War Museum 19 (B), 27 (B), 29 (B); Leyland Vehicles Ltd 26 (T), 28 (B), 30 (T), 31 (both), 32 (both), 34 (T), 36 (both), 37 (all), 38 (both), 40 (B), 41 (B), 49 (both), 51 (B), 52 (both), 53 (B), 54 (B), 55 (both), 56 (both), 58 (T), 63 (both), 64 (B), 65 (T), 66 (D), 67 (both), 68 (T), 68 (C), 69 (B), 71 (T), 72 (B), 80 (T), 82, 83 (B), 85 (both), 86 (B), 87 (both), 88 (B), 89, 91, 94, 95 (both), 96 (both); Ministry of Defence (Army) 88 (T), (Procurement Executive), 84 (B) (Royal School of Military Engineering) 84 (T); Pandoro 80 (B); National Freight Corporation 74 (T), 76 (B), 77 (both), 78 (both), 79 (B), 81 (T); Rolls-Royce 53 (T); Seatrain Mideast 81 (B); 600 Group/Lignacite Products 61 (B); Tor Line 80 (C); Robert Wynn & Son 65 (B), 73.

First published 1982

ISBN 0 7110 1173 7

Published by Ian Allan Ltd, Shepperton, Surrey, and printed in the United Kingdom by Ian Allan Printing Ltd at their works at Coombelands in Runnymede, England.

Above: A ballast-bodied heavy haulage Tractor built during early 1950s on a Scammell Mountaineer chassis of the type that was originally designed as an all-wheel-drive vehicle for the construction industry.

Contents

Above: A Wyn's Crusader with a typical 1980's style
'out-of-profile' item for shipment.

Introduction

A popular dictionary defines the lorry as 'a large strong open truck or wagon'*. Had the compiler added that it might be required to carry dry goods, bulk liquid, or steel pipes, through crowded city streets, across deserts, on unmade logging tracks, or along high-speed motorways, he might have conveyed a more accurate impression of its versatility, but whatever the definition there can be no escaping that basic requirement for *strength*.

'Industry' – an equally broad description of the lorry user – has become accustomed to asking its truckbuilders for extra tractive effort, and as it has sought the capability to haul general cargo payloads of up to 50 tonnes, so too has it demanded off-highway performance that it can bring to bear on the problems of haulage in the developing nations, and in the construction and extractive industries as well as in the traditional heavy and site haulage markets. That these requirements are not irreconcilable is confirmed by the number of major truck manufacturers offering users in all sections of the market the operational advantages of a rationalised product range. Inevitably though there is a need for specialisation, for although they might incorporate many of the same components as their cargo-carrying counterparts, dump trucks, loggers, oilfield self-loaders, and military and civilian heavy haulage tractors need not only sufficient strength for their specialised roles, but must often be designed 'from the wheels upwards' to meet the specific requirements of the sector of the market for which they are destined. In terms of vehicles employed, each of these sectors compares poorly with the volume 'goods' end of the market, but taken together they comprise a fiercely specialist market – a tough, mechanically demanding commercial battlefield in which the name Scammell commands respect.

Scammell's status is a classic demonstration of the merits of building on strength. Scammell & Nephew originally built up its wheelwrights and coachbuilders business at Fashion Street in London's decidedly unfashionable Spitalfields late in the Victorian era, but by the outbreak of World War 1 in 1914, with much of its attention focussed on steam wagons and light trucks, it had already acquired something of a reputation as an innovator. Like many of the early automotive engineers, Scammell – by that time guided by Lt-Col A. G. Scammell and his brother – was quick to capitalise on the lessons learned by military transport operators during the four years of war, and in 1919 developed its first articulated combination. Articulation was still a new concept when in the following year its prototype demonstrated its potential by climbing West Hill,

Highgate, in second gear with an 8ton payload, and attaining a creditable 18mph on level road, yet the response was sufficiently encouraging to prompt Scammell to move its works to the more suitable site at Tolpits Lane, Watford, that it occupies to this day.

Scammell Lorries Ltd was formed on 1 July 1922 nine months after its prototype tanker combination had been unveiled at the Olympia Motor Show. The use of a fifth-wheel coupling and the imposition of a load directly onto the rear axle of the tractor unit made the articulated outfit particularly suitable for the haulage of bulk liquids, and early support from Shell-Mex Ltd encouraged the newly-formed company to concentrate a substantial part of its efforts on tanker construction. By the late 1920s specialisation was beginning to pay dividends. The rectangular tank of the prototype gave way to a round tank on a rigid frame, and when this was in turn superseded by a lightweight frameless design which permitted a commensurately higher payload, tanker combination sales increased to account for around four out of every five vehicles leaving Tolpits Lane.

Articulated and rigid eight-wheeled tankers continued to make up a substantial proportion of Scammell's output for nearly 40 years – although by the end of that time the emphasis had shifted to the provision of a cost effective eight-wheeled chassis rather than a complete vehicle. In 1927 however, the introduction of the rugged six-wheeled chain-driven Pioneer, an off-highway heavy haulage tractor signalled the start of an entirely new specialisation. With a superior cross-country performance derived from a rocking-type front axle, and 2ft of vertical movement at each rear wheel, Pioneer found a ready market amongst operators in the oilfields and logging forests, and in so doing provided a cornerstone of the company's fortunes throughout the economic gloom of the early 1930s. Nevertheless it was the more conventional cargo carriers which made up the greater part of the order book. Scammell was already an established force in the heavy and off-highway sectors of the market, and although there can be no doubt that its reputation for strength and durability earned there was instrumental in its winning a larger share of the general haulage market, it is equally certain that a high level of cargo vehicle sales was essential for the support of engineering and development at Tolpits Lane.

This interdependence between the mainstream of production and the specialist activities remained a feature of Scammell's activities until Leyland's 1980 development of a rationalised product range defined the role as being solely that of specialised vehicle constructor. At that stage, the ubiquitous Routeman eight-wheeler accounted for almost two-thirds of the 1,500 vehicles per year output,

* The Penguin Dictionary (Penguin Books Ltd).

and its own somewhat specialised position as a heavy-duty tipper clearly owed much to the 'tough' corporate image. Routeman epitomised interdependence, but there had been other mainstream activities less obviously linked to the 'heavies'. Foremost amongst these was the Mechanical Horse, introduced in the mid-1930s as a means of securing a share of the fast-growing urban delivery and service vehicle market, and which remained a viable concept for more than 30 years – during which time it produced sales of more than 20,000 tractor units, and 100,000 trailers.

Whilst the Mechanical Horse provided Scammell with a third complementary stream of producton, a new generation of diesel-engined maximum payload general cargo vehicles had begun its progress from the drawing board, and although some new models had already been introduced, the outbreak of World War 2 interrupted the evolutionary process at a point at which it seemed that substantial benefits were likely. Thus wartime vehicle production at Watford was confined to Pioneer variants and the mechanical horse, and although the latter was widely used at storage depots and base installations – and its coupling fitted to thousands of Bedford tractor units – it was Pioneer's wartime reputation for rugged reliability that provided the stimulus for a higher degree of specialisation in the heavy haulage and off-highway sectors at the war's end.

In the early 1950s, an article attacking the 'Scammell Myth' appeared in the Corps journal of the Royal Electrical and Mechanical Engineers, written by an officer who had clearly found reliability a poor compensation for the lumbering Pioneer's weight and lack of speed. Argument flared briefly and then subsided. There was no myth; the Scammell was basically a 12-year old design that had done all that had been expected of it. By the 1950s when it was still in widespread service it fared less than well in some comparisons with its powerful US-built contemporaries, but if the fault lay anywhere it lay with the War Office for having failed to order a state of the art vehicle. To prove their point, Scammell enthusiasts pointed to the latest Mountaineer and Constructor types, both of which were proving outstandingly successful in tough export markets, and both of which retained most (if not all) of the features which had made Pioneer such a commercial success in an up-dated layout.

'Strength to spare' and its inevitable weight penalty, and adherence to well-proven design principles are Scammell characteristics that have on occasions earned Watford-built heavies a 'too-conservative no-frills' tag. The reality is of course that if a design is to be capable of adaptation to any one of a variety of tough tasks 'strength to spare' is a primary requirement, and the design longevity that it bestows a valuable management tool for both manufacturer and customer alike. Adherence to established technology is not only prudent for a manufacturer of Scammell's size, but also reduces logistic and operational problems for vehicle users, many of whom are necessarily operating their vehicles in remote environments.

In its production mainstream – dominated throughout the 1950s and 1960s by a new generation of maximum legal weight 'trunk'-type vehicles – Scammell often blazed a pioneering trail. Both the Michelotti-designed glass-fibre cab, and the Crusader premium tractor were in many respects well ahead of their time, but in the final reckoning Scammell's future was determined by the policy of its Leyland parent, and the eventual assignment of the 'specialist' role came at a time when the UK domestic truck market was in danger of being swamped by a tide of heavily-promoted European imports. Inevitably there were casualties within the Leyland group. AEC, Thornycroft, and Guy all slipped from view as their traditional markets were eroded and Leyland grasped around for an effective response. By contrast, Scammell, stripped of what might have been an embarrassing product range, with profitable global markets for its military and specialist vehicles, and with leadership in the UK eight-wheeler sector with its Routeman model, possessed obvious strengths around which Leyland's planners could build for the future. Unlike some of its luckless partners the Watford concern survived, a name to reckon with in its chosen areas of specialisation, and synonomous with reliability whenever the going was tough.

Inevitably the Scammell story is one of trucks at work. Surprisingly perhaps for a company with more than 60 years of history, there have been relatively few models, but as the photographs on the following pages show, all have been adapted to a variety of roles, which together span the entire haulage spectrum. Some will be remembered for hauls that 'outsiders' thought impossible. Others merely as reliable workhorses. All had that quality of strength that the dictionary compiler considered to be so important.

Acknowledgments

Many people have helped me to assemble the Scammell story. Much material would have been beyond reach had it not been for the whole-hearted co-operation of Leyland Vehicles Ltd, and especial thanks are due to Alan Wheatley, Scammell Motor's own Publcicity Manager for his assistance at a time when there were a great many pressures being brought to bear on the entire organisation. Similarly, my task was made much easier as a result of the efforts of Mr A. J. Staley, who as Secretary of the National Freight Corporation volunteered much useful information on the vehicles used by the corporation's operating subsidiaries. Library staffs at both the Imperial War Museum, and the National Motor Museum took pains to provide me with material that I needed, and I am particularly indebted to Mr S. W. Stevens Stratton of Ian Allan Ltd for access to material in the *Modern Transport* archives. Of the many Scammell operators contacted during my research, mention should be made of Robert Wynn & Son (Mr John Wynn), English China Clays, and ARC Ltd (Mr David Badney), who like the various departments of the Ministry of Defence were most generous with their assistance.

To all of them, and to my many friends in the the Road Haulage industry who have provided so much valuable first-hand advice and assistance, I am most grateful.

1 1923-39 Evolution

Above: The original 1921 chain-drive six-wheel articulated tank unit in service with the Crow Carrying Company six years after its first registration, by which time the original three-speed gearbox had been replaced by an improved four-speed unit, and its engine uprated. The 2,000gal frameless tank shown here was also an improved version of the original with an 11-12ton payload. The sale of 14 such vehicles to Shell Mex in 1923 established a link between the two companies that was to endure for more than 50

years, and placed Scammell in the forefront of suppliers to the oil industry. By 1925, Scammell had developed a frameless tank specifically for oilfield use, which could be detached from its tractor and winched to the well-head on a bogie whenevery conditions were impassable for road vehicles. In the same year a blower unit was developed to speed the discharge of bitumen and other heavy liquids.

Left: The versatility of the six-wheeler was demonstrated by its 1925 adaptation to the cable-carrying role. In the meantime however several hauliers had successfully put Scammells to work on a variety of specialised haulage tasks. This 1922 articulated outfit was used by a London contractor to deliver heavy radio-telegraphy equipment. Vehicles of this type were fitted with four-cylinder petrol engines developing 75-80bhp and three or four-speed gearboxes. Final drive was via heavy roller chains running from an intermediate jackshaft with a differential gear, and readily exchangable jackshaft sprockets enabled drivers to gear their vehicles to suit the conditions likely to be encountered on each journey. Payload of this particular vehicle was 7½ton, and its maximum speed 12mph.

Above: Scammell designers also developed a number of tractor/trailer combinations for other specific applications. The brewing industry, although still faithful to its dray horses for urban deliveries had a need for a higher payload lorry for its longer hauls, and specially bodied vehicles were supplied to several major concerns including Surrey-based Friary, and Allsopps.

Below: The shape of things to come. 1927 saw the first Pioneers trundle out of Tolpits Lane, rigid six-wheelers designed to operate wherever the going was tough, and developed with overseas markets in mind. Inevitably, the oil companies were early customers for the newcomer, and the vehicle seen here on trial with a load of tree trunks was destined for a pipeline contract in Iraq, where off-highway performance was all-important. A pivoted front axle, with rocking 'balancer' beams secured to a chassis by semi-elliptic springs at the rear permitted any of the wheels to rise by as much as 2ft without twisting the frame. It was a formula that was to serve Scammell and their customers well for many years.

Above: As an off-highway pipe carrier, Pioneer could operate at gross weights of up to 100ton. In every respect a 'giant of its day' the 80bhp tractor unit had a single driven rear axle, optional four or five-speed gearboxes, a pedal-operated transmission brake, and a handbrake operating on all wheels.

Below: A 1932 Pioneer cross-country cargo carrier demonstrating its capability on a 1 in 2 sand gradient prior to shipment to Australia where it was to be put to work in the goldfields. Like all Scammells of its day, Pioneer made its debut fitted with the well-tried four-cylinder ohv petrol engine, and it was not until 1932 that the Gardner diesel was offered as an alternative to the in-house unit. The six-wheeler's superb cross-country performance soon attracted the attention of military users, but although sales were made to India and Japan, the British authorities remained generally unconvinced until the mid-1930s.

Above: The years 1929-31 were despite the prevailing economic gloom, something of a watershed for Scammell, and there was no more spectacular development than that of the 100ton heavy hauler – seen in this instance in 1946 at the head of a giant transformer en route from Stafford to Nottingham. There was however nothing revolutionary about the Watford heavyweight, which like so many of the vehicles that were to follow it exemplified the Scammell philosophy of remaining faithful to a well-proven layout and building 'extra' capacity into a design. Thus the 80bhp engine was retained – albeit coupled to an eight-speed gearbox – together with chain-drive and solid tyres, but the matched 65ton capacity trailer incorporated a newly-developed steerable rear bogie. The control wheel for the latter – which is visible at the rear of the trailer – was operated by a pedestrian steersman who had a telephone link to his driver. The 100-tonner was one of those vehicles which could not be kept out of the headlines, and numbered amongst its more notable hauls, the steel girders that were to frame London's Cumberland Hotel, and a 95ton whale washed ashore during a storm.

Right: Scammell's range of conventional cargo trucks also took a significant step forward in 1929 when the new four-wheel six-tonner made its debut at Olympia at the Commercial Motor Show. Powered by the 'usual' 80bhp petrol engine, but without chain drive, the 6-tonner also had a 17ft×7ft 6in cargo body on a 17ft Wheelbase chassis which enabled it to carry both volume and weight. The chassis was specially constructed for use with 40in×8in pneumatic tyres and twin rear wheels, suspension was by semi-elliptic leaf springs, and the braking system comprised a transmission brake with a 16in drum and 19in front brakes, both operated by a pedal, and lever operated 19in drums on the rear wheels. Although primarily a goods vehicle, the four-wheeler was capable of adaptation to specialist roles, and 24in of articulation on the rear axle made it a particularly attractive proposition for work involving unmade roads or undeveloped sites. In 1931 Scammell demonstrated their continuing commitment to the specialist sectors of the market by offering the four-wheeler as the basis of a mobile concrete mixer. The elevatable 2.3cu yd drum, developed by Transit Mixers Ltd of London, was driven through a power-take-off.

Left: Although by 1929 the entire Scammell range with the exception of the 100-tonner and a 15-17ton articulated unit had been converted to run on pneumatic tyres, there were still many solid-tyred types in service. This early-1930s picture of part of Thomas Allen Ltd's Stanford-le-Hope based fleet shows solid-tyred 12ton six wheelers, some with discharge blowers mounted in front of their engines, alongside pneumatic-shod ten-tonners fitted with 40in×8in tyres and coupled to five-compartment tank units.

Right: By 1930 there were already more than two hundred frameless Scammell tank units in service on UK roads, and from 1931 vehicles were available with welded aluminium 3,000gal tanks produced by Thompson Bros of Bilston. That year's Commercial Motor Show model was destined to be operated by Crow Carrying on behalf of Somerlite Ltd, and could carry either 3,000gal of kerosene or 2,500gal of motor spirit. Earlier in the same year Scammell unveiled an articulated eight-wheeler for trunk cargo operation at the UK maximum legal weight of 14tons. The new model could however operate in overseas countries at up to 17 tons, and superseded the solid-tyred 15ton combination introduced four years previously. After only two years the 17-tonner was itself replaced by what was in effect a new vehicle specifically engineered to be able to accept a diesel engine.

Centre right: This Mendip Transport 15ft wheelbase six-wheeler of 1931 vintage, but with an 11½cu yd/10ton hopper body, displays many of the prominent characteristics of its predecessors, and was clearly a product of the 'if you've got a good idea – stick to it' school of thought.

Below left: Another newcomer in 1931, the six-wheeled 12-tonner had a 19ft wheelbase, and a 22ft × 7ft 6in cargo body. The 80bhp petrol engine was retained, and drove the forward bogie wheels via a five-speed gearbox, a differential countershaft, and Duplex chains. 13.5in × 10in low pressure tyres were fitted as standard equipment, and the rear suspension consisted of semi-elliptic springs oscillating on a central trunnion.

Above: Enter the diesel. The 88bhp Scammell petrol engine was the product of more than 12 years consistent up-grading and by the late 1920s already incorporated such refinements as Specialloid alloy pistons, a Claudel-Hobson carburettor with three choke tubes, Duralumin con-rods, raised compression ratio, and improved Simms magneto. However operators were beginning to

favour 100bhp diesel power units, and from 1932 onwards the RC138 12tonner had the 102bhp Gardner 6LW available as an off-the-shelf option, and began a relationship in which the names of the two companies were to become almost synonomous. With an overall length of 30ft, and a capacious body, the six-wheeler became a firm favourite with trunk service operators, and was soon to be seen sporting a variety of open and tilt bodies.

Below: Whitbreads' Fleet No 1. A 1934 lightweight 13-tonner with bodywork and cab by Strachans (Acton) Ltd, an unladen weight below six tons, a Scammell petrol engine, and a six-speed gearbox. Both the six-wheeler and its articulated 15ton stablemate had epicyclic double reduction final drive and compressed air braking systems.

Above left: The four-wheeled six-tonner with an 88bhp version of the petrol engine was selected as the basis of a small batch of fire engines ordered by the Borough of Watford in 1933 as part of a campaign to support local industry during a time of severe economic depression. The height of the chassis – normally 3ft 1in – was dropped in order to provide a low loading line, and a 400/700gpm capacity two-stage turbine pump installed.

Left: Although the mid-1930s found Scammell vigorously developing its general cargo and tanker designs, development of specialist heavy vehicles derived from the Pioneer design was never neglected. One project of particular interest was the 1934 oilfield tanker produced for the Anglo-Iranian Oil Company. The two vehicles were powered by 160bhp Parsons petrol engines, and fitted with 10-speed gearboxes, Gruss air springs, and double reduction drive axles, but although the concept was one of the most advanced of its day somewhat surprisingly it was never developed into a production model. It is perhaps unfortunate that this should have been the case as the Iranian special seems to have been comparable in most respects to some of the big US-built tractor units.

Top and above: Scammell also produced a number of specialist workshop vehicles for the Newcastle-upon-Tyne Electric Supply Co based on the solid-tyred version of the articulated 12-tonner. These vehicles were remarkable for the range of heavy equipment that they carried in their low-frame trailer units, but despite the ingenuity of the design it was essentially a 'one off' and not seriously exploited.

Top and above: A second specialist type produced for the same customer incorporated a self-loading demountable body system mounted on a standard rigid 12-tonner chassis. Cargo could be carried to sites in three separate box-like body sections, each of which could be lowered to the ground and recovered by means of a winch and retractable tail-mounted ramp.

Above: Pneumatic tyres had greatly enhanced the six-wheel articulated combination's versatility, and for some applications, Scammell tractors were coupled to specialised trailers developed by other manufacturers. William Kenyon & Son of Dukinfield, nr Manchester, produced one such unit, an insulated tank for the carriage of hot bitumen, which used their patent interlocking panel, galvanised sheet metal insulation system and a 4in sandwich of slag wool to maintain the contents in a liquid state.

Below: An early Pioneer loading an infantry tank whilst on trial with the British Army. The articulated semi-trailer version of Pioneer offered to the War Department at the time of its introduction, was ordered in Limited quantities as a recovery vehicle for disabled tanks. However the complementary jib-crane equipped breakdown vehicle, and the Heavy Artillery Tractor version were not ordered until several years later (almost too late for the start of World War 2), by which time the RAOC tank recovery teams equipped with Pioneer had discovered its knock-out rear bogie to be anything but a 'knock-out' in the field.

Top: The Mechanical Horse – introduced to the public at the 1932 Motor Show – was an exciting new project which opened fresh markets for Scammell which eight years previously had made an unsuccessful foray into the delivery vehicle sector with their ill-fated Autovan. Like the Autovan, the Mechanical Horse was an unconventional vehicle, but its role was to be eminently practical. As its name suggested, the three-wheeled tractor unit seen here in prototype form, was intended to replace the horse, and having been designed to be able to draw modified horse-drawn drays it seemed assured of a good reception as urban carriers awoke to the advantages of mechanisation. Eventually the type developed into a remarkably powerful urban load carrier but as first produced the 20mph three-tonner was powered by a 10hp side-valve engine driving via a single plate clutch, four forward plus reverse gearbox, and a double reduction rear axle with a readily exchangeable final drive ratio.

Above: The first Mechanical Horse models were available in both three and five-tonner versions, the latter having a more powerful 2-litre engine as an option. Both were fitted with instantaneous coupling gear which enabled a driver to spot and drive on to a parked trailer, and drive away without alighting from his cab. It was a capability that made the Mechanical Horse particularly suitable for work at docks, goods depots, and rail terminals, where it could pick up trailers delivered by long-distance articulated units, and either shunt them or undertake short delivery trips. By 1934 when this frameless tank outfit was delivered to Crow Carrying, the more powerful version had been uprated to 6-tons, and was being increasingly used for specialist applications in addition to its more customary general haulage and tanker roles.

Above: A hydraulically-operated tipper version of the six-tonner developed in 1934, and powered by an uprated four-cylinder petrol engine was one of several Mechanical Horse variants demonstrated to municipal authorities for use on congested routes. The remarkably inexpensive-to-run Mechanical Horse tractor unit could be coupled to a wide range of specialist trailers, and its versatility had an obvious appeal to users with a diverse seasonal workload.

Below: Nevertheless there was a considerable demand for the drop-frame general freight body, and this Thomas Allen 'seven-wheeler' was developed for a pioneering roll on-roll off service. In such a role, a tractor unit would normally work three trailers on a 'one loading, one unloading, and one in between' system. As a conventional cargo trailer, the drop unit had a 2ft 4in loading height, and a 15ft × 7ft 3in load space.

Top left: A 3ton municipal refuse carrier had been amongst the earliest configurations proposed for the Mechanical Horse, and within three years of its introduction the range had been developed to include a 12cu yd trailer with a Scammell-developed moving floor, and a 1,250gal version of the familiar frameless tank adapted for kerbside washing/sprinkling. The City of Westminster vehicle was operated by the Highways Department as a 3ton street maintenance tender (note the 'plate' giving details of carrying capacity, mounted above the front wheel).

Centre left: The mechanical street washing unit was a developed version of the tractor fitted with rotating brushes, but employing a high proportion of standard Mechanical Horse driveline components.

Left: A late-1930s version of the MH3 3-tonner in service as a conventional cargo carrier. In 1937 Scammell also introduced a battery electric 4-tonner which was externally similar to its petrol-engined counterpart, but powered by a 9.5hp electric motor and two Exide batteries (which weighed an awesome 15cwt). A foot operated controller gave four forward speeds.

Above: The introduction of the first eight-wheeled rigid 15-16 tonner in 1937 opened yet another long chapter in the Scammell story. The eight-wheeler was already a familiar sight on British roads, but the Scammell was unique in having its front axles carried on their own frame which was in turn located by an arrangement of radius rods and suspended by rubber columns – a configuration that conferred obvious advantages on say humped-back bridges by sharing the load between all four front wheels instead of imposing it all on the leading axle. The Gardner 6LW diesel was selected as standard equipment, as was an epicyclic rear axle, and a constant-mesh six-speed gearbox.

Above and below: The six-wheeler was still going strong, as may be seen from this 1938 high-sided cargo truck in the red and black livery of the Post Office Stores Department. This essentially 1930s design makes an interesting contrast with the more economic eight-wheeler as typified by the Barlow vehicle. Road haulage was rapidly assuming a new significance in the world of commerce, and its needs could only be met by a new generation of maximum weight load carriers. However their introduction into service was to be delayed.

Above and below left: The eight-wheeler with a 3,400gal insulated edible oil tank and three-cylinder discharge air compressor displays many features that were still to be in evidence on vehicles in the late-1950s. The Bibby vehicle has single rear tyres, and the well-proven Scammell rubber suspension similar to that used on the articulated vehicles of the day, but operators were also offered the option of twin tyres and steel-spring rear suspension as on the brewery flats operated by Watford brewers Benskins.

Above: The outbreak of World War 2 in September 1939 brought the first part of the Scammell story to an abrupt end. There was little or no time for the development of new models, and for the next five years Tolpits Lane and the nearby Moor Park trailer factory – opened in 1940 – were kept at full strength meeting the demand for military versions of existing vehicles. It is a period that is perhaps best remembered as the heyday of the Pioneer's military descendants, and there is no doubting that Scammell's years of perseverance with the big tractor – often in the face of official indifference – were amply justified. The 'Heavy Brigade' led the way, but the mechanical horse went to war too, in a variety of roles, one of the earliest of which was as a mobile decontamination unit equipped to cordon off areas affected by poison gas, and to mop-up in the wake of a gas attack.

Centre left and left: The *Commercial Motor* ended its account of the Scammell exhibit at the 1937 Commercial Motor Show with the remark 'We must not conclude. . . without making reference to the Scammell gun tractor. This is an interesting machine powered by a 102bhp Gardner oil engine'. In the years between 1939-45 such interesting machines acquired an altogether new place in the order of things.

Scammell in common with most other manufacturers had developed new products to meet the demands of the three services and the authorities responsible for civil defence. One such vehicle was an adaptation of the Mechanical Horse as a very basic fire fighting vehicle equipped with water tank, ladder and hosereels, and towing the heavy duty trailer pump which was to figure prominently in Scammell's output during the war years.

Top: Although Scammell had offered the military an artillery tractor version of the Pioneer in 1927 it was 1936 before the first orders were placed. The R100 Heavy Artillery tractor, seen here during its acceptance trials was equipped with 'overall chains' which fitted over the 13.50 tyres on the rear bogie to enhance cross-country performance. These chains could be stowed in the 'cargo compartment' of the trials vehicle, but would normally have been carried in a locker beneath the off-side of the cab. Power was provided by the familiar Gardner 'six', and from 1938 onwards, the R100 was fitted with a Scammell-designed vertical spindle winch.

Above: There were few British manufacturers in a position to deliver a tank transporter 'off the peg', and although both Scammell and Albion produced tractor/semi-trailer combinations the latter was soon downgraded leaving the Pioneer-derived outfit as the sole home-produced vehicle in the 30ton category. Altogether, 548 transporters were delivered to the Army between 1939-45, and although they were all nominally 30-tonners, they were used extensively to transport the 31ton US-built Sherman tank. The Scammell was however the ideal transporter for the generally lighter British-built Cruiser tanks, and as heavier and more specialised types of armoured vehicle were introduced towards the end of the war, the 102bhp 30-tonner became outnumbered in service by the heavier US-supplied 185bhp Diamond T. The low-loader type of semi-trailer with a knock-out bogie was superseded by an improved end-ramp type early in the war.

Right: The Artillery Tractor was a bulky vehicle, and by no means easy to manoeuvre in tight corners, but although it was acquired primarily as a prime mover for the army's 17½ton 7.2in howitzers it was also used to tow engineer plant trailers. In addition to its three seater cab it could accommodate a nine-man gun crew in a steel-panelled main body. A hinged tailgate was provided to facilitate loading ammunition and equipment, and there was also a 10cwt chain operated hoist on a roof-mounted steel gantry to assist in handling heavy howitzer shells. Total production of the R100 during the war reached 786 units.

Below: One artillery tractor which did not enter service however was the 4×4 petrol engined coastal artillery haulage tractor designed to an Admiralty specification, and delivered as a prototype six months before the outbreak of war. With the exception of some specialised rail guns, coastal artillery remained an Army responsibility, and the project was shelved, leaving the single tractor vehicle to eventually pass into the hands of a fairground showman. Powerful as it was, the 4×4 lacked the cargo-carrying versatility of the R100, and AEC's broadly comparable 4×4 Matador.

Below right: The recovery vehicle derived from Pioneer was known to the military as Tractor Heavy Breakdown 6×4 Scammell, and was numerically the most important component of the Watford plant's wartime heavy vehicle output. Two variants were produced, namely the SV1T fitted with a collapsible-jib crane (of which less than 50 saw service), and 2,000 SV2s, similar to the vehicle shown here kitted out for issue from an ordnance vehicle depot. Both versions were fitted with the Scammell 8ton vertical spindle winch, but the SV2 had a sliding-jib crane which could be extended from its travelling position to long and short lift positions at which it could lift 2 and 3 tons respectively. With its slow revving diesel engine, distinctive front-mounted ballast weights, and radiator 'kettle' the Scammell wrecker was a familiar vehicle wherever the British Army served for many years after the war and as recently as 1980 the last of the wartime SV2s was reported to be still in service with the Army's Belize garrison.

3 Mountaineer and Constructor. The New Breed

Above left: When the end of the war signalled the resumption of commercial vehicle production at Tolpits Lane, one of the first significant batches of specials to leave the works were these oilfield platform trucks, 4×4s with 18ft platform bodies destined for Colombia. The design was unremarkable and in many respects a restatement of the principles which had made the prewar 15-tonners so successful, but the use of four-wheel drive provided a clear pointer to the direction in which Scammell considered its future to lie.

Below left, above and below: Other versions of the early postwar 4×4 were equipped as tankers, off-highway tippers, and gin-pole equipped oilfield transporters, all of which were to become familiar configurations to the Scammell designers in the years ahead.

Above left: The Mountaineer range, which began to leave the production lines in 1949 was a logical 'next-step' from the type of vehicle supplied for the Colombian contract, but its introduction marked a significant increase in the company's commitment to the on-off highway sector of the market. Mountaineer shared many components with the six-wheel Explorer tractor developed concurrently against a military requirement, but the four-wheeler had a more flexible specification which permitted its use as a cargo vehicle – as evidenced by this stake-sided version which sold well in African and the Middle East throughout the early 1950s. This particular vehicle was one of a number purchased by the Crown Agents in their capacity as purchasing agents for colonial administrations.

Left: Mountaineer was primarily a heavy hauler designed to operate in the toughest environments, yet requiring none of the specialist skills that were often needed to operate the heavier types of vehicle. Power was provided by a 10.35-litre 130bhp Scammell-Meadows diesel driving through a six-speed gearbox to double reduction driving axles. Suspension was by semi-elliptic springs, with the transverse lay-out at the front providing as

effective a Scammell trade-mark as the name above the radiator. *Dolly Ann* with her outsize load on an unmade road through the forests of British Guiana typifies Mountaineer at work – a hauler built for the developing nations.

Top and above: Mountaineer's versatility made it the ideal vehicle for oilfield operators who had hitherto been compelled to use either expensive 'one-offs' or modified versions of World War 2 heavy-duty tractors. Although there was little to excite in Mountaineer's strictly conventional layout, it was easy to operate and maintain, and its versatility meant that an operator could standardise on the Watford-built truck throughout his fleet – a factor which further eased the problem of maintenance in the field. This adaptability is well demonstrated by the two versions shown here awaiting delivery to the Middle East; one is a winch-equipped oilfield flatbed, very much a standard piece of desert hardware, the other an articulated tractor/trailer combination used for long-hauling supplies. Both have four-wheel drive and the high ground clearance so essential for off-highway use, yet despite the different configurations there was virtually complete component commonality.

Left: An oilfield flat, identical with that shown on the previous page, but far from Tolpits Lane in service with the Kuwait Oil Company. Vehicles of this type could self-load skid-mounted items by winching them on to the low superstructure mounted behind the cab, and could also if required to do so use their gin poles for other lifting tasks. This 1954 photograph emphasises Mountaineer's excellent ground clearance characteristics.

Below left: Although Scammell enjoyed an enviable reputation as tanker specialists, the tankers destined for the oilfields were a far cry from the Highwayman based vehicles that were a familiar sight on roads nearer home. This Kuwait Oil Company vehicle mounted on the 4×4 Mountaineer was fitted with massive tubular fenders, and its own fuel tank was protected against accidental damage by a tubular cage.

Above right: Mountaineering the Libyan way! A 1954 photograph of a late-series Mountaineer ploughing its way through soft sand in the Libyan desert illustrates the sort of conditions that the big trucks were expected to take in their stride. Later Mountaineers were fitted with a redesigned front wing which afforded more protection than the original cycle types. The cab fitted to Mountaineer, and later to Constructor brought a new standard of comfort to off-highway vehicles that was to endure for more than two decades. There was still an absence of all but the bare essentials, but the high mounted cab provided the driver with a far more satisfactory working environment than some earlier vehicles in which forward visibility had been too restricted for off-highway work.

Below: Later versions of Mountaineer could be fitted with any number of alternative power units to suit the particular application for which the vehicle had been ordered. Inevitably there were

Gardners – an ever-present on the Scammell specification sheet – at 112 and 150bhp, and after Scammell's merger with Leyland a 150bhp 'in-house' unit, but the introduction of a new range of Rolls-Royce diesels widened the choice still further.

The 4×4 Recovery version developed for use in extreme off-highway conditions was powered by a Rolls-Royce C6NFL developing 150bhp at 2,100rpm, and fitted with Reynolds Boughton recovery equipment. A jib crane could undertake suspended tows of up to 5ton, and a heavy-duty ground anchor enabled the vehicle to perform heavy winching tasks with its 15ton vertical spindle winchgear. The tyres on the vehicle illustrated – which was destined for the Abu Dhabi Defence Force – were 24×20.5 Sahara developed by Michelin for desert use.

Whilst Scammell in common with most British industry turned its sights to export markets, a construction boom got under way in the United Kingdom, and the 1950s saw the start of numerous major projects which were to provide the feedstock and energy for new technologies. Marshland was reclaimed to provide sites for refineries, and barren moorland transformed into the sites for new power stations. Site works on such a scale opened new markets to Mountaineer, as a need for increased levels of productivity led to the development of new techniques and equipment. Mountaineers were duly modified to carry newly-designed high-capacity concrete mixing machinery, and to provide the basis for scow-bodied dump trucks. The site dumper requires a sufficiently strong chassis to withstand the repeated shocks of loading from excavating machinery, as well as the ability to force its way through hub-deep glutinous mud. That Mountaineer was so frequently chosen for such work reflected the wisdom of the Scammell policy of deliberately designing their vehicle with far higher tolerances than would at first sight seem to be necessary.

Above: Mountaineer also provided the basis for some of the first postwar genuine heavy haulage tractors, and replaced veteran R100 'ex-servicemen' and prewar outfits in the fleets of several specialists. This ballast-bodied 60-tonner had a 14ft wheelbase, and was constructed to the specification of Middlesex transport contractors Everley Bros during the late 1950s as a tractor for heavy drawbar trailers.

Left: It is only fitting that the section of this book devoted to Mountaineer should conclude with a picture of the truck in the environment for which it was designed. In some respects the 4×4 is the least-well remembered of the Scammell heavies, having been often overshadowed by the feats of its more highly-rated successors. Yet it was Mountaineer which led the way into the off-highway market at a time when the truckbuilding industry was retooling itself for a new attack on world markets, and the reputation that it earned – particularly in the oilfields – had a significant bearing on the development of new models.

Below left: Although Mountaineer continued to win sales successes, it was the new Constructor which proved to be the star of the 1952 Commercial Motor Show. That a vehicle rated as a 100-tonner should have such exceptional off-highway performance was due to its newly-designed rear bogie, and to the replacement of the inter-axle differential by a system of independent drivelines to the second and third axles, each of which was anchored through ball mounted tie rods arranged to counter propshaft movement during axle articulation.

Above: A 1953 Constructor awaiting delivery to Steel Engineering Ltd. It will be noted that this vehicle lacks the external air filters fitted to later versions, and is fitted with an un-louvred engine cover. Constructor was the first commercial vehicle to be fitted with the Rolls-Royce C6NFL diesel, which in its developed form produced 185bhp at 2,100rpm with rated torque of 505lbf at 1,200rpm. An independently mounted six-speed gearbox in combination with a high/low transfer box gave the 6×6 12 forward speeds, whilst the winch – apparently not fitted to the Steel Engineering vehicle – could be operated in six speeds.

Below: Like its Mountaineer predecessor, Constructor had to earn its reputation the hard way, hauling the needs of the Middle East oilfield operators across a terrain that made no concession to weaknesses in either man or machine. It was an environment in which the 'abnormal' – even this 260ft length of pipe – was the norm, and progress was often so slow that a man might have walked faster. But Constructor had been designed with the desert in mind. An air-spaced canopy helped to keep cab temperatures at a more acceptable level, and extended forward to provide a visor. Engine air was drawn through massive filters, and there were shields to protect the brake mechanism from abrasive dusts – yet astonishingly, Constructor still relied on the same undamped transverse leaf front suspension that had been fitted to its Pioneer forerunner.

Above: The end of a long haul. A typical scene from the mid-1950s as a driver begins unloading his winch-equipped Constructor outfit on arrival at a desert drilling camp. Comment on the standard of loading seems at first sight to be superfluous, but Constructor was a 60ton plus hauler, the desert was restriction free, and a driver's skill could be measured by his ability to get the right weight distribution for conditions that could vary from hard-packed sun-baked sand to wind-blown shifting seas of fine particles.

Below: Self-loading. A 1958 photograph of a Constructor using its winch to load a generating set at a remote desert site. The standard oilfield flatbeds, and oilfield equipment trailers were fitted with tail and side rollers to facilitate the loading of heavy items of equipment at locations where there were no suitable cranes available. Constructor was equipped to handle skid-mounted items of up to 30ton in weight.

Above: Not all oilfields are in the desert, and when in 1955 Shell was developing its Seria field in North Borneo, it found that there was a need for a wrecker that could traverse ground made impassable to all but specialist vehicles in order to carry out heavy winching work. This vehicle built by Harpers of Guildford on a Constructor chassis was the first of its kind to be completed in the UK, and its equipment fit was centred on a twin-jib crane housed in a specially designed steel body reminiscent of those fitted to US-built World War 2 wrecker trucks. The cab-roof mounted spotlights and air horns were optional items on Scammell's specification sheet, but were regarded as essential by the men in the field.

Below: Constructor's versatility was such that it was eagerly seized upon by specialist hauliers in many fields who were anxious to re-equip their fleets with state of the art tractor units. Demand increased steadily too as Rolls-Royce progressively developed its C6NFL to the stage at which it eventually delivered 210bhp (and 570lbf torque at 1,400rpm). Scammell responded to the demand with the Junior Constructor, a 6×4 version aimed principally at the on-highway sector of the market. Inevitably there was a good response from the heavy haulage contractors. The 1959 vehicle supplied to North London hauliers Silbermann was typical of the many such trucks taken into service for specialised hauls.

Above: The Constructor with a rear axle rated at 40ton could be readily adapted for such roles as that of the motive power unit for a mobile drilling rig, in which capacity it could be driven cross-country to a site, and quickly jacked up for use. Such vehicles which were extensively used in the construction industry for trials borings, as well as in mineral and oil exploration operations, were fitted with auxiliary engines to power drilling equipment. The drill derrick was erected at the rear of the tailgate.

Left: Although it possessed both power and off-highway capability, Constructor failed to attract significant interest amongst builders of airfield fire-fighting equipment. However, Shell – which had good reasons for its confidence in a type that had served it well in a variety of roles – ordered this 1961-built crash-fire-rescue vehicle for use at a company-operated airfield in Venezuela.

4 Highwayman, Handyman, Routeman and Trunker

Above: Whilst the 'heavies' notched up sales throughout the world, designers at Watford has been hard at work on the next generation of less dramatic load carriers. The big bonnetted 30ton Highwayman tractor had been introduced in the mid-1950s as an obvious follow-on from earlier designs, and special versions had been developed to meet the requirements of the oil companies which were now permitted to carry up to 4,000gal of petroleum spirit on UK roads in a single load, but were still not allowed to exceed a 22ton gross weight limit. A considerable amount of ingenuity went into the design of what was at first sight a bulky truck. The stepped frameless tank had five compartments each of which held the legal maximum of 500gal, but nevertheless it was still possible to fit a pump for discharging loads other than petrol and still remain within the weight limit.

Below: Amongst Highwayman's predecessors had been this attractively-styled 4,300 US gallons capacity tanker combination exhibited at the 1952 Commercial Show. The 15ton payload outfit was powered by a 132bhp Meadows diesel, and was clearly an elegant piece of 'kite-flying' for it does not seem to have attracted a great deal of serious interest. Certainly when it eventually emerged, Highwayman was a far more practical vehicle with better forward visibility, and a tank unit that was far more appropriate to the realities of bulk plant operation.

Above: Subsequent versions of Highwayman incorporated a new-style cab with a number of weight saving plastic components, wrap-around windscreen and automatic trailer-coupling equipment. Rated at 24tons GCW, the late-1950s Highwayman was powered by a Leyland 0.680 diesel developing 161bhp. Following the company's absorption by the Leyland Motor Corporation in 1955, Scammell eventually became the group's specialist division, and although some of its subsequent vehicles hardly qualified as special types, Highwayman's particular suitability for the petroleum industry probably earned it the 'specialist' tag.

Left: Handyman 1, a 24ton GCW tractor which made its debut in 1960 was a forward control version of Highwayman with a dimensional set-up which enabled it to haul trailers of up to 27ft in length – the then legal maximum length on UK roads. Like its bonnetted counterpart, Handyman had a cab which incorporated a high proportion of plastic components, and the 0.680 diesel driving via a six-speed gearbox and double reduction axle, but its 8ft 6½in wheelbase enabled it to keep within the 35ft limit when hauling longer types of trailer.

Right: In 1960, Scammell unveiled its eagerly-awaited new eight-wheeler but Routeman had been designed in accordance with the Scammell practice of sticking to what appeared to be a winning formula, and was arguably too heavy and not sufficiently ambitious in concept. Nevertheless the 'eight-legger', which was marketed in both 8×2 and 8×4 forms embodied all the qualities of reliability that went with the name, and sold well particularly to tanker operators. The 1962 vehicle shown here was one of a fleet of 41 Scammells operated by United Molasses, and was fitted with 2,600gal capacity tank, automatic lubrication, and pto and pumpgear.

Centre right: A Routeman 1 Powder tanker destined for General Refractories of Sheffield nearing completion at Tolpits Lane. This 1961 vehicle was fitted with the standard 140bhp Leyland diesel, but the 150bhp Gardner was available as an option.

Left: A glassfibre cab designed by Italian body-stylist Michelotti was the outward sign of the arrival of Routeman 2. An extensively revised specification included power assisted steering, a chassis/cab weight below six tons, and the Leyland diesel driving through a six-speed gearbox to the rear bogie. At the time of its introduction the restyled Routeman had a basic price of £4,215, and its principal appeal was still to tanker and general haulage operators, although Scammell had begun to canvass its claims as a suitable vehicle for tipper operators. The 1964 Routeman 2 illustrated here formed part of a Yorkshire-based fleet employed on the distribution of steel strip products.

Above: In the years that followed, the 24ton GVW Routeman was progressively up-dated, and in 1964 was fitted with the developed version of the Leyland 0.680 power unit – albeit downrated to deliver 185bhp at 2,100rpm. BP Chemicals operated a fleet of Routeman tankers, one of which is seen here leaving its Salt End (Hull) plant early in 1968.

Above: In 1960, Scammell had produced three pre-production examples of its proposed Trunker maximum legal weight tractor unit, but unlike Routeman they had incorporated some significant departures from accepted practice. Trunker 1 was a 6×4 forward control powered by a horizontal Gardner 6HLX 150bhp engine mounted behind and beneath the cab at frame level, and driving through a six-speed Scammell gearbox mounted ahead ot it. The drive was turned through 360-degrees by a set of gears, and transmitted to the leading driven axle by a shaft running beneath the engine and gearbox. The double-drive rear bogie had double reduction axles in a non-reactive four spring layout. Of the three vehicles produced, one went to Scottish hauliers McKelvie, and another to BP, but when Trunker appeared as a full production model in 1965 it did so in Mark 2 form as a more conventional

32ton 6×2 twin-steer – a type known in the industry as a 'Chinese Six' – sporting a cab generally similar to that fitted to Routeman 2.

Below: Trunker 2 – as typified by this 1966 vehicle operating in conjunction with a frameless tandem-axle tank trailer – was powered by the Leyland 200bhp engine with the lower-rated Gardner again available as an alternative. The second steering axle had a bellows mechanism at each of its spring centres in which pressure was maintained at 70psi during normal running. If the driver began to lose traction in adverse conditions, he could obtain better adhesion by releasing air, and transferring weight to the driving axle.

Top: This tandem-axle tipper combination illustrates how Trunker's Michelotti cab was set back over the front axle in order to avoid frontal overhang – a feature which lost it many friends amongst drivers mounting and dismounting on cold wet nights! From 1966 onwards, Trunker was offered with an optional semi-automatic transmision comprising a five-speed Self Changing Gears RV38 epicyclic gearbox and splitter mechanism. Like several of its contemporaries, Trunker 2 was plated at 35ton in anticipation of the elusive legislation that manufacturers and hauliers hoped would increase legal weight limits within the UK.

Above: Trunker 3 was introduced in 1970 at a time when there was a growing interest amongst hauliers in a tractor capable of drawing the new types of trailer used for transporting ISO freight containers. Such trailers had a considerable overhang, and in its 'long' configuration, Trunker was particularly suited to the task. The improved Mk 3 vehicle was equally suitable for bulk haulage jobs where there was a need to accommodate a considerable volume within a limited trailer length, and another feature which attracted interest was the Dunlop Maxaret anti wheel-lock equipment available as an 'optional extra'.

Left: A 220bhp Rolls-Royce engine was an attractive alternative to the standard 200bhp Leyland unit, but there was a hint of increased rationalisation within the organisation in a drive line which now included the BL range change gearbox, and Leyland Beaver hub-reduction axle.

Below left: Handyman too was progressively updated throughout the 1960s and the Mark 3 version which first appeared in 1964 was fitted with the all-plastics Italian-styled cab – but like Trunker with over the wheel entry and exit. Handyman 3 had originally been designed to meet a British Road Services requirement, but although it was purchased in considerable numbers by the state-owned haulier, its concern with operating economically led to a specification which attracted a number of major customers from the private sector of the industry.

Above: Trunker's 6×4 configuration had however fitted it for a variety of specialist tasks, one of which was as a high-capacity airfield refueller for the Chevron Oil Company.

Below: The refueller was not bound by the Construction and Use Regulations which limited the size of vehicles permitted to use UK roads, but another Trunker variant developed for brewers Whitbread & Co might well have had a future as a mid-range cargo truck. The one-off platform bodied six-wheeler was without the characteristic Trunker twin-steer, but otherwise combined the best features of that vehicle with those of Routeman, and although it is said to have performed well in service it seems to have sunk without trace for no other reason that that quantity production would have conflicted with similar vehicles produced by other Leyland companies.

Right and centre right: Handyman 4 continued in production until the mid-1970s, when what some experts saw as a long-overdue review of the Leyland product ranges reduced Scammell's output to only its more specialised vehicles. Routeman was to survive as a workhorse for the 1970s but Handyman and Trunker were axed. They were essentially trucks for the 1960s neither particularly comfortable nor highly powered by the standard of the rising generation, but nevertheless state-of-the-art haulers which performed reliably and economically in fleet use.

Below: In 1968, before Handyman fell victim to the rationalisation programme, Scammell had made what turned out to be a last attempt to broaden the base of its marketing effort in the 30/32-tons GCW category by adapting Handyman to suit the requirements of a wider section of the market. The MK 3 model featured the same six-speed AEC gearbox as the Routeman, the 200bhp Leyland engine, and increased front brake area. For the Mk 4 which made its debut three years later, Scammell retained in-house diesel, gearbox, and hub-reduction rear axle, but permitted purchasers the option of either a 220bhp Rolls-Royce or 180bhp Gardner engine.

A low unladen weight permitted ECC Quarries to fit a blower motor to its dry powder tankers without seriously affecting their payload, however, some imported tractor units were already being fitted with comfortable sleeper cabs, and although the authorities still frowned on their use, Handyman's more austere interior became a very dubious asset.

5 Crusader and Routeman. Workhorses for the 1970s

color photo on dust jacket.

Left and below: A Crusader 6×4 Tipper operated by Cubitts Ltd and a tanker supplied to the Taylor Woodrow construction group for use in Nigeria. The premium tractor's fundamental ability to run for long periods with minimal maintenance and reduced driver fatigue, coupled with a high payload made Crusader a particularly economical proposition in demanding environments. Yet in many respects Crusader – Scammell's last trunk vehicle, and perhaps a victim of circumstances – remained an underestimated machine which never realised its full potential in what had been intended as its primary role.

Above: In the late 1960s, British Road Services developed a specification for a maximum weight hauler most suited to what it foresaw as its needs during the 1970s. Mindful of their previous experience with Handyman the state-owned haulier approached Scammell with a view to tailoring its new Crusader to its requirements. Coincidentally, Scammell had anticipated a domestic demand for a high-cab tractor unit designed for maximum vehicle utilisation, and eventually made no fewer than 22 prototype Crusader 4×2s available to BRS for intensive testing over their long haul routes.

Trials lasted for two years, and although the 280bhp Rolls-Royce Eagle 2 performed well, BRS eventually opted for a normally aspirated 220bhp version of the engine for their vehicles. Both engines were offered to UK hauliers, and the two Crusaders eventually lined up alongside each other at the 1971 Scottish Motor Show, where the BRS version was seen to have a somewhat less well-appointed cab, but a wheelbase 3in longer than that of the 280, automatic lubrication, and a 10-speed range change gearbox.

Below: Although it was a vehicle for the 1970s, the 220 was designed with traditional UK operating conditions in mind. The more powerful 280 drew extensively on Scammell's experience of overseas markets in an effort to satisfy the requirements of a generation of hauliers whose interests lay in tightly scheduled operations and on international long-hauls. The turbocharged Rolls-Royce Eagle produced 265bhp nett at 2,100rpm and torque of 785lb ft at 1,400rpm, comparable with most imported vehicles, but still noteworthy by UK standards of the day. A nine-speed Fuller RTO9509A overdrive gearbox and Leyland hub reduction gearing were standard equipment, and the makers claimed a 'low stress' maximum speed of around 56mph.

Surprisingly in view of the needs of the section of the market for which it was intended, Crusader 280 did not have a sleeper cab option available at the time of its launch. The deficiency was remedied in time for the 1972 Commercial Show, but it can have done little to establish Crusader's credibility as an international long hauler.

Above: Crusader 220 as a tractor for a maximum weight tipper combination. UK legislation permitted tractor/trailer combinations of up to 15m in length, and 32.514 tonnes (32ton) in weight. Crusader found favour with operators for applications with few restrictions on the size of vehicle, and good conditions in which to load and unload. Amey Roadstone used this outfit to make deliveries of powdered limestone from one of the West of England quarries from 1973 onwards.

Below: Despite their initial impact, the 4×2 Crusaders gradually lost their standing in the sales league, and almost inevitably became a casualty of the drastic changes through which Leyland Vehicles hoped to retain its share of a market that was in danger of being swamped by imported high-cab trucks. Should Crusader have been given a new lease of life, or was Leyland right to have persevered with its own-badge Marathon premium tractor? With hindsight it is possible to see the logic of the rationalisation process which led to the demise of the Watford-built 4×2, (ironically its place in the assembly hall was to be taken by Marathons assembled on behalf of Leyland Vehicles), but at the time the issue was an emotional one. This cut-away illustrates quite clearly why at the time of its 1971 introduction Crusader 280 was widely regarded as a pacemaker in a section of the market that was just waking up to the shape of trucks to come. However its kerb weight – 6.35 tons – was more than one ton heavier than that of the highly competitive Volvo F-86, and when legislation to raise the UK legal limit above 32.5 tonnes failed to materialise, this differential began to take its toll of Crusader's domestic sales.

T. Grisley

Right: On the export front though, the 6×4 version had made consistent headway from the time that the vehicle pictured here had signalled Crusader's debut at the 1968 Commercial Show. The high gross weight market was beginning to develop remarkably quickly, particularly in Africa and parts of the Middle East, but unlike some of its competitors, which were scaled-down machinery carriers, Crusader was a tailormade premium hauler well-suited to the needs of hauliers operating on some of the world's toughest routes.

Above: Powered by either a Detroit Diesel 8V71N turbocharged V-8 developing 288bhp, a 305bhp Rolls-Royce Eagle, or a 350bhp Cummins, the 6.5tonne tractor unit could be supplied in a variety of configurations for use in the 44.3/66tonne range. The 44ton tandem drive rear bogie had a lockable third differential, and a 15speed Fuller RTO915 gearbox was fitted as standard equipment. Despite several 'cosmetic' up-dates, the late-1970s models as typified by this 65ton GCW heavy tractor, incorporated the same Motor Panels cab as its predecessors, and although not fitted as a full sleeper could be fitted with a drop-down bunk.

Top: A haulage version of the Crusader 6×4 destined for service in West Africa coupled to a Crane Fruehauf general cargo trailer. Crusader sold well in those markets where the heavier Scammells enjoyed a long-standing reputation for reliability in tough operating conditions. Throughout the early and mid-1970s though there was an ever-present possibility that yet another policy change within the Leyland organisation might mean that the products might lose their identity and be re-badged as Leylands. The recurrent suggestions that such a change might be imminent drew loud protests from overseas distributors, for there was a certain strength implicit in the Scammell name which provided Crusader with a far more effective selling line than any advertising copywriter could have devised.

Above: The Australian long-distance haulage scene is one of the world's toughest, and most leading European, US, and Japanese truckmakers are prepared to fight fiercely for a share of it. In 1972 Scammell produced a specifically 'Australian' 32ton GCW version of Crusader employing the same drive train as the standard 6×4 but dispensing with frame flitching, and fitted with higher frame members and fabricated spring brackets in an effort to cut weight. Paradoxically many hauliers sought lightweights so that they could fit a full range of extras essential for survival in the outback. The Ansett outfit pictured here is fitted with an air-conditioned sleeper cab, and other extras appropriate to its long distance role including rock-guard, 'kangaroo-catcher', spotlights, and long-range fuel tanks.

Left: Because of its high gross operating weight, Crusader could be comprehensively equipped, yet still retain capacity for a thoroughly acceptable payload. Thus the combination illustrated here comprised a 6×4 tractor unit coupled to a high-sided trailer fitted with a high-capacity hydraulic loader. The versatile Crusader continued to attract fresh customers as it entered the 1980s amongst whom were the Russians who evaluated a long-haul version on the long haul between Moscow and principal cities in Iran.

Bottom left: Not the least of the 6×4's many roles was as a heavy haulage tractor for loads of up to 150 tonnes gross weight. The 100CR 100ton (101.7 tonnes) version shown here was powered by a 305bhp Rolls diesel, and when fitted with the standard 7.12:1 rear axle ratio could negotiate gradients of up to 1 in 7.17 (13.95%). The unladen tractor had a wheelbase of 4.267m (14ft) and weighed 10.262 tonnes. Its rear bogie was rated at 32.5 tonnes, and the 15-speed gearbox was the same Fuller unit as fitted to the bonneted Contractor – which generally had a lower top gear maximum speed, but superior gradability.

Right and below: Recovery version of the 4×2 Crusader produced during 1980 for Leicester-based recovery specialists Unity, and subsequently operated on behalf of a Scammell distributor. The extended-wheelbase tractor unit was powered by a 290bhp Rolls diesel, and fitted with recovery equipment built around a Holmes 655 extendible-boom wrecker. Scammell proposed several

recovery versions of Crusader of which possibly the best known was the military vehicle fitted with Swedish EKA equipment (qv). The 6×4 was also offered with the all-British Recoverer equipment-fit. The Holmes 655 Power Wrecker fitted to the United vehicle could handle all types of passenger car and most heavy duty towing jobs. The extendible booms could be used for industrial work at lengths of up to 18ft, and with both in use, the unit was rated at 16 tons.

Above: Question. When was a Crusader not a Crusader? Answer. When it was an Amazon. The Crusader 100ton heavy haulage tractor was originally to be known as Amazon, but for reasons that are unclear the Thornycroft type name was dropped in favour of the CR100 designation. However a number was delivered to international heavy haulier Robert Wynn & Sons Ltd which retained the name and as on this 1978 example en route to that year's Motor Show – displayed it beneath the radiator grille. Wynns began its relationship with Scammell during the inter-war years when it operated a night trunk service between South Wales and London as well as a heavy haulage business, and subsequently operated Watford-built heavies wherever it has had major contracts.

Below right: Introduced at the 1970 Commercial Motor Show, Samson was an early attempt to up-rate the Crusader series for heavy haulage tasks of up to 75ton gross weight. In order to permit loadings of up to 27 tons on the fifth wheel coupling, a second steering axle was accommodated within a 13ft wheelbase frame, 4ft 3in ahead of the first driving axle, and the depth of the frame beneath the coupling increased to 18in.

In this 8×4 configuration, Samson had almost the capacity of Contractor – which at that time was capable of accepting an imposed load of only 30 tons when operating at 20mph – and enjoyed the considerable advantage of component interchangeability with other Crusader models. However despite two years testing in Australia, Iran, South Africa, and Europe, Samson soon faded from view, and the single example was acquired by Pickfords which retained it in service for nearly a decade. Six generally similar vehicles were specially built by Leyland Australia during the early 1970s, using components supplied by Scammell.

Top right: Routeman 3 was Scammell's big seller throughout the 1970s and by 1979 with the Marathon premium tractors built for the Leyland parent company accounted for two-thirds of the output from Tolpits Lane. The off-highway and heavy haulage trucks had added greatly to the company's reputation, but Routeman was the volume-seller which brought Scammell's

particular expertise as specialists in vehicles for the toughest operating conditions to bear on a rapidly expanding sector of the UK market. Tipper operating is a savagely competitive business, and the 30ton GVW twin-steer eight-wheeler is a uniquely British vehicle, built to conform to equally unique legislation, but in the early 1970s the growing demand for aggregate, mineral, chemical, and animal feedstuff tippers attracted the attention of several prominent manufacturers from mainland Europe. Inevitably the newcomers provided most of the excitement in the market, backing cut price offers with new and enthusiastic dealer networks, but Routeman 3 powered initially by an 11.1-litre Leyland engine generating 202bhp, and subsequently by the 209bhp turbocharged T11 unit which developed 605lbf ft torque at 1,300rpm retained market leadership until it was eventually phased out of production at the end of the decade.

Above: A 1973 Routeman 3 collecting a load of aggregate from ARC's Theale plant. Although suitable for a number of applications, it was a tipper that Routeman earned its new lease of life, giving Scammell an opportunity to participate in the bulk transport boom of the 1970s, and to retain a substantial share of the domestic market at a time when its future within the Leyland organisation seemed to be at its bleakest.

Above: A late model Routeman 3 in a typical working situation delivering roadstone near Queensferry in October 1978. Routeman was available with a choice of 18.8tonne or 19.3tonne rear bogies, with hub reduction axles to reduce half-shaft stress in the demanding conditions in which tippers often have to operate. Payloads were extremely good by the standards of the day, and when fitted with its standard six-speed constant mesh gearbox and 6.93:1 rear axle Routeman had a a maximum speed of 53.10mph, could climb a 17.54% gradient, and restart on a 14.4% slope.

Below: As major producers of concrete aggregates and roadstone, the Amey Roadstone Corporation needs vehicles which have the traction to cope with the mud and slime that are inseparable from quarry operation, but remain highly productive in the high-frequency shuttle between plant and site. Routeman formed a vital part of ARC's fleet throughout the 1970s, and in this photograph, a 1978 model is seen leaving the company's Shoreham plant with a load of sea-dredged aggregate. Routeman earned the reputation of being very much of a 'bosses' motor', and although admittedly its glassfibre cab eventually fared none too well in comparisons with those of its contemporaries, its operating economy, and lifetime cost were never seriously contested.

Left: 'Lifetime' for a Routeman often seemed to defy the odds. A convoy of Routeman 3s travelling along the private haul road linking English China Clays' twin ports of Par and Fowey. A typical working day for the trucks in the Cornish-based group's china clay fleet might have involved either repeated trips along the haul road, or a succession of tedious unladen climbs to the clayworks on the high moors inland followed by a brake and transmission testing descent to sea level loaded with up to 20 tons of processed clay. In either case, the day would have been punctuated by loading and tipping in a penetrating haze of white clay dust; it was a tough routine, yet many of the vehicles remained in service for up to 11 years.

The longevity of the ECC Scammells was by no means exceptional. A second-hand Routeman about to be pensioned off from a major operator's fleet invariably attracted a queue of would-be purchasers, and a glance at the vehicles at any tipping contract would normally reveal numerous Scammells enjoying an extended working life in the hands of owner-operators.

Below: Fleet owners too found ways of further extending the operational life of their Routeman 3s. Lignacite Products, having decided that delivery of their structural blocks by tipping truck was outmoded, took a six-year old Routeman, extended its wheelbase by 24in and its overall length by 72in, and added a new sub-frame. A HIAB hydraulic loader was then mounted amidships, and a body comprising two 13ft high-sided compartments suitable for carrying banded blocks added. The conversion cost Lignacite around £10,000, but when it was complete they had a refurbished Routeman with an 18.5ton payload doing a job which might otherwise have cost them £30,000 for a new vehicle.

Heavy Transport (ECC) Ltd is responsible for servicing the total transport needs of the English Clays group, and its fleet necessarily includes both long and short distance cargo carriers as well as the tippers which support production operations. By fitting Routeman tippers with a fully-demountable swap-body system, Heavy Transport was able to extend its capability. The system which permits the driver to exchange bodies within three minutes without leaving his cab freed the eight-wheelers from their dedicated tipper role, and also meant that they could be operated more efficiently in situations where slow filling processes or shortage of ancillary plant might otherwise have led to long periods of waiting time.

6 Super Constructor and Contractor

Above: Super Constructor was a name first heard in 1956 applied to a Constructor fitted with a 200bhp version of the Rolls C6NFL engine. In other respects the vehicle had differed very little from Constructor, but by 1960, the developed 6×6 had evolved as a very different vehicle with significant points of difference from its forerunner – which at the stage it complemented rather than superseded. The new Super-vehicle was fitted with an automatic eight-speed gearbox, and a completely re-designed suspension system in which the transverse leaf at the front was replaced by a transverse beam with helical springs and dampers at either end, and the semi-elliptical springs at the rear discarded in favour of a solid beam pivoted directly onto the chassis frame. The vehicle illustrated is a very early Super Constructor supplied in 1959 as the tractor for a 15-20ton oilfield flat.

Below: In tractor form, Super Constructor could be rated at up to 100ton GCW. The rigid oilfield flat – the vehicle shown in this picture was destined for BP Trading – could operate at up to 49 tons (49.79 tonnes) – but retained the capability to climb a 37% (1 in 2.7) gradient, and to restart on one of 34% (1 in 3). Super Constructor retained Constructor's switch-in all wheel drive, and its revised rear suspension provided 12in of fore and aft, and 17in cross-articulation.

Above: Later models of Super Constructor featured a revised
offset two-man cab, and eventually by the mid-1970s a 275bhp
version of the C6TFL. The designers stayed loyal to the
Constructor's individual drive line to each driven axle concept,
but as a glance at this late-series BP oilfield rigid shows, the type
had evolved into a remarkably specialised vehicle. Super
Constructor was sold outside the oilfield and construction
industries as a military recovery vehicle, and as a general purpose
heavy hauler, but examination of some of the standard equipment
available for the oilfield role reveals the extent to which Scammell
had developed this particular specialisation.

With overall dimensions of 35ft 6in × 9ft × 10ft 4in (high),
the 26ft 3¾in wheelbase Super Constructor was a large vehicle by
any standards. Its high payload, and cross-country capability
alone were sufficient to earn it a 'specialist' label, but in order to
be able to compete for a share of the profitable 'desert oil' market,
a 'loaded' specification was essential. Thus the tropicalised timber

floor of the flatbed was steel-decked for two-thirds of its length,
and sockets were provided for carrying drill-pipe stanchions, as
well as tail lashing points, and fitments necessary for the erection
of the internally reinforced gin poles. A Darlington Model 70
22.3ton winch was usually fitted, and a 'headache rack' above it
was fitted with guide rollers, and tubular extensions for supporting
gin poles.

Below: 1964 saw the launch of the Contractor family of heavy
haulage tractors which had been specifically designed as a solution
to some of the more complex haulage problems in the developing
countries of the world. The prototype shown here was rated at
38ton GCW, but the range was intended primarily for tasks in the
region of 100ton gross weight. Contractor's 240bhp Cummins
NH250 diesel was a reflection of the growing global authority of
the US diesel manufacturers, and was coupled to an eight-speed
semi-automatic transmission and a 16ton rear bogie.

Top: The Contractor range comprised seven basic models, suitable for the bulk tipper, recovery, heavy haulage, heavy general haulage, road train (162.5tonne), logging, and machinery transport roles, and included both 6×4 and 6×6 variants. As the range developed, a fully automatic Allison transmission became available as an alternative to the standard 15-speed Fuller range change gearbox, and the engine option to which either could be matched was uprated to either 335 or 425bhp. As an ultra-heavy hauler as illustrated here, Contractor was usually fitted with the Cummins KT450 turbocharged diesel/Allison CLBT750 combination, and a range of specialist equipment including a massive tri-level towing hitch four-door crew cab and a ballast body built to the customers specification.

Above: 'Superior' by name, and superior by nature. A Contractor Mk 2 operated by Robert Wynn & Sons, fitted with the 450bhp engine, and automatic transmission comprising torque-converted lock-up clutch, five-speed gearbox, and hydraulic retarder. An auxiliary four-speed gearbox was used with restricted torque input for very low speed manoeuvering. Contractor's suspension system consisted of a longtitudinal semi-elliptic leaf spring layout at the front, with trunnion-mounted semi-elliptic springs at the rear. The rear axles were of the spiral bevel type with epicyclic hub reduction, and the bogie was fitted with a lockable third differential.

Above: One of the least likely roles for Contractor was as the basis of a passenger coach. Fifteen 21ft 8in wheelbase chassis were supplied to South African State Railways during the mid-1960s for fitting with locally-built bodywork, and used for passenger services and light goods delivery in mountainous areas. A Cummins NH220 rated at 212bhp provided the power for what must have been one of the most substantially-built PSVs ever to have entered service.

Below: Although Contractor was capable of adaptation to a number of off-highway tipper roles, cost considerations normally limited its use to the more specialised tasks associated with minerals extraction and refining. The booming market in the Gulf States during the 1970s opened up a number of fresh possibilities for heavy vehicle manufacturers, whose local market had hitherto been largely restricted to the desert oilfields and allied activities. The two Contractors awaiting shipment to Qatar, were ordered by a concrete products manufacturer for use in conjunction with Dyson semi-trailers at a gross weight of 86.36tonne (85ton).

7 Scarabs, Sherpas and suchlike

Above: Most of the action in the Scammell story is inevitably provided by the big tractors and off-highway haulers. Nevertheless it is perhaps somewhat unfair that space considerations compel the grouping together of the postwar successors to the Mechanical Horse with the highly specialised dump trucks produced since 1945, since each was an exceptional performer in its own right.

Scarab – the three-wheeler – was certainly no mere stay-at-home and ought to be remembered by more than the 'railway parcels delivery' tag. Introduced at the 1948 Commercial Show it featured a combined engine/gearbox/rear axle unit mounted behind the cab, and was rated in the case of the 6tonner at 45bhp at 3,200rpm. The more modestly powered 25bhp at 3,200rpm. The more modestly powered 25bhp 3tonner had a double reduction final drive providing an overall ratio of 9.65:1, and both had shackleless semi-elliptic springs bearing on bracket-mounted slippers for their rear suspension, and an oil-immersed coil spring at the front. Scarab was of course designed to sell Scammell trailers too, and both straight and drop frame trailers were produced for version.

Right: By 1954 when this 3-tonner was photographed in a typical African scrubland, Scarab had been made available with an uprated 34bhp four cylinder petrol engine. This particular vehicle was powered by a Perkins diesel – possibly the 42bhp 4.99 – but most early diesel options were taken up by UK users of the 6-tonner which was available with a 52bhp Perkins as an alternative to the standard petrol engine. The braking system of the semi-trailer automatically engaged itself when the tractor unit was coupled, thereby ensuring a quick turnround whenever the vehicle returned to its base.

Left: Scarab found particular favour with brewers as a versatile and highly manoeuverable replacement for their traditional drayhorses. The 'three-tun' trailer awaiting collecting in this 1954 photograph of pre-Christmas activity in the despatch bay of a wellknown brewery was a familiar part of the city scene which will be remembered with affection by a generation of Londoners who remain unconvinced of the merits of some more recently developed brews.

Right: There will no doubt be many ex-servicemen who will be similarly moved by the sight of this fleet of 6-tonners operated by Malta-based brewers Farsons in the mid-1950s. The 16ft 6in semi-trailers were of a type known as a brewer's body – a description that might have been equally well applied to the condition induced by their contents!

Below right: Although very much a 'basic' vehicle that afforded its occupants scant comfort, Scarab nevertheless attracted the attentions of the specialist bodybuilders. This Whitson-bodied version was supplied to the South London Brewery in 1949, and incorporated several airflow and infill features which were being canvassed as a means of improving fuel economy nearly 30 years later. However the trailer gives the impression of having been difficult to load over its sides, and its use might have entailed the sacrifice of some of the accessibility that was one of Scarab's operational advantages.

Above: Like its predecessor, Scarab was a popular vehicle with municipal authorities, who found that its manoeuverability and operational economy made it most suitable for urban start-stop-start work. This 1958 tipping refuse collection outfit had a capacity that seems to be less than economic when judged by the standards of a later day, but for the time – before the packaging revolution increased the amount of discarded materials – such combinations were judged to be most effective. Scarab could be of particular value where an authority needed a vehicle to support street cleaning gangs that could be readily adapted to the gritter role in winter months.

Below: Similarly the tractor unit could be coupled to any one of a variety of specialised trailers – as for example this gulley emptier in service with a Danish municipal authority.

Below: Scarab, said its critics, was uncomfortable. There was a need for a new generation of light articulated vehicles, which combined the comfort of contemporary 1ton vans with the traditional virtues of the Mechanical Horse. Scammell responded to the challenge by co-operating with another Leyland group company Standard, to produce the Scarab-Four which combined the cab of the new Standard 'Twenty' forward control 1ton pick-up and its 2.26-litre Leyland OE138 diesel with Scarab running and coupling gear. The resultant vehicle – although unashamedly hybrid – had superior roadholding, braking, and stability but was not intended as a replacement for the three-wheeler.

The light articulated outfit was however moving towards the end of its career. Scarab Four was only a limited success, and Townsman – unveiled in 1965 – with an improved glassfibre cab and slipper spring suspension was, although a far more

satisfactory three-wheeler, essentially a vehicle for British Railways with a future that was almost inseparable from that of an organisation that was soon to divest itself of its road haulage interests. The new National Carriers concern assumed responsibility for the mechanical horse fleet, but the type's future was already in considerable doubt as most manufacturers were producing a far more comprehensive range of light commercials, and Leyland appeared to have decided that its limited appeal did not accord with their plans for a production mainstream composed of volume sellers.

So the mechanical horse faded from view – arguably never to be adequately replaced – a low cost delivery vehicle that had become too costly to produce. Such shifts in marketing policy had become part of everyday life for truckbuilders, but whilst the mechanical horse was being phased out, fresh requirements were developing.

Right: One of the new developments was a scow-bodied dump truck which combined off-highway capability with a chassis, suspension, and body capable of withstanding repeated heavy shocks. Mountaineer had already been adapted for such a role – the vehicle illustrated here was one of a number operated by a prominent contractor during the 1950s – but its two-man cab and bonneted configuration was a compromise design that was not acceptable to some operators looking for a purely off-highway vehicle for mining and quarrying work.

Above: The Scammell solution for the late 1950s was Sherpa, a more specialised forward control one-man cab 20-tonner which made no pretence of being an on-highway vehicle, but which was nevertheless not too large to be driven on public roads when exceptional circumstances arose.

Left: Sherpa was designed to be capable of being readily fitted with specialist bodywork to equip if for a variety of roles. This 1963 example was one of a batch of three supplied in kit form to an Indian manufacturer, who fitted them with locally built rock-carrying bodies.

Right: In 1959, the 6×4 Himalayan made its debut as an off-highway 30.5tonnes GVW dump truck powered by the 200bhp Power Plus 0.680 engine and fitted with Sherpa-type one-man cab. Himalayan's off-highway performance made it particularly suitable for other roles than site dumping. One was as a chassis for mobile cranes, and the vehicle shown here was one of a batch of three fitted with Jones KL44 crane equipment for mobile heavy lift work at an Indian steelworks.

Above: The mergers and reorganisations within Leyland Vehicles eventually led to Scammell assuming responsibility for several specialist vehicles formerly manufactured by other companies in the group. Two of these were the LD24, an AEC-designed Dump Truck capable of operating at 27.69 tonnes GVW, and the closely related LD55, a Bush Tractor rated at 66.06 tonnes GCW (design maximum). Both were extremely rugged trucks designed to work away from surfaced roads, and in environments where as one Scammell man put it 'daily maintenance was just washing out the cab with a hose.' LD55 was also developed as a Dump Truck with a payload of up to 14.0tonnes. A Leyland AV760 engine developing 212bhp and 5641bf ft of torque (the latter at 1,300rpm) provided the dumper with its power driving via a constant mesh five-speed gearbox.

Although it was a dual-purpose vehicle, not a best-seller, and by no means as specialised as some quarry dumpers, the 6×4 LD55 attracted considerable interest, and remained part of the Scammell range throughout the period that rationalisation was taking its toll of some of its more highly-publicised stablemates. A batch was supplied to the British Army in response to a requirements for a vehicle which could maintain convoy speed on the road as well as being capable of operating as a genuine site vehicle. In such applications, the limited payload of the Scammell's dump body was no drawback. Productivity for such vehicles depends on the length of the haul, and the number of loading shovel passes required to fill the body, and the expensive high capacity loaders are more likely to be found on mining sites, than on military engineering works.

8 The Heavyweights.
Postwar Heavy Haulage Tractors

Below: Wynns of Newport had been amongst the earliest customers for the 'rigid six' 12-tonner when it was introduced in the early 1930s. Nearly 40 years later it was still buying Scammells, but like Pickfords, another major user of the Watford-built trucks, it had become internationally recognised as specialist in the movement of heavy indivisible loads.

The work was tough, tedious, and demanding of the highest standard of man and machine. Often – as was the case with the outsize piece of refinery plant being hauled ashore at a Thames-side site by a ballast bodied Contractor of 1971 vintage – the load was too heavy for transport on public roads, and as the years passed other manufacturers entered this specialised market with their own heavyweight tractors. Nevertheless for many road users it is the image of a pair of close-coupled Scammells at the head of some piece of gargantuan hardware that comes most readily to mind at the mention of 'abnormal load ahead'.

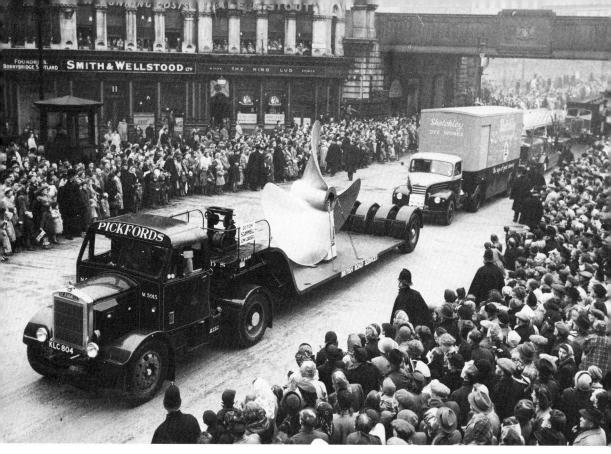

Above: In 1949 however a 20ton machinery carrier was still regarded as something of a heavyweight, and warranted a place in the Lord Mayor's Show. The 4×2 Tractor was powered by a 102bhp Gardener diesel (although a 130bhp Meadows engine was available as an alternative) which drove via a six-speed gearbox. The low-loader semi-trailer was fitted with a knock out rear axle. A small batch of this particular type was supplied to the Royal Navy.

Below: Show business is one thing, real life is another altogether grimier business. A 1948 photograph of a prewar machinery hauler operated by Kinder's Transport. Solid-tyred, and chain-driven, some of these veterans served on until the late 1950s.

Above: London-based heavy haulage specialists E.W. Rudd Ltd operated this early R100 based tractor unit during the late 1940s. The load is a 70ton transformer en route from Walton on Thames to London's Victoria Docks.

Below: For the most part, heavy haulage during the early postwar years was still the preserve of the ex-WD Pioneer derivatives, and upon their 'demobilisation' the 30ton tractors and wreckers were eagerly siezed upon by hauliers and construction companies where there was a need for pulling power. That many were still running 20 years later came as no surprise to the generation that had driven them across Europe and North Africa on active service.

Above: Nor were the ex-military vehicles confined to the UK in their new role. Wherever the going was rough, there was a better than average chance that you would find a Scammell. When Gailey and Roberts of Nairobi wanted to move a 42ton excavator along a 72-mile journey across Kenya's heartland, they hired an ex-World War 2 recovery tractor operated by Mowlem Ltd to do the job. The excavator is being re-loaded after crossing a dried-up river bed on its own tracks during the course of the four-day haul.

Below: By 1951, new heavy tractors like Mountaineer had arrived on the scene, but most were despatched to foreign parts as part of the postwar export drive. In any event why replace a vehicle when it's running well? Pickfords still operated a number of solid-tyred chain-driven specials of the 1930s as exemplified by this 100-tonner pictured near St Albans in January 1951 carrying a diesel locomotive from Newton-le-Willows to Tasmania via the Festival of Britain exhibition held that year on Westminster's South Bank site.

Top: There are indivisible loads, and there are indivisible loads. If you have to move the world's largest sheet of plate glass from St Helens to the South Bank exhibition, there must be times when you wish that your load was somewhat more indivisible – particularly when you find yourself with the prospect of having to pull across tramlines and a patch of LCC-style pavé within a few hundred yards of your destination. A British Road Services Gardner-engined 15-tonner and trailer on Westminster Bridge in December 1950. The use of rubber in the rear bogie suspension unit fitted to Scammell semi-trailers had been one of the company's major innovations during prewar years and at least in part accounted for the longevity of some of its products.

Above: In April 1954 a Britannia aircraft on a test flight from Bristol Aircraft's Filton works made a forced landing on the nearby Severn Beach. Pickfords provided Scammell-style muscle for a hastily assembled recovery team, which also included agricultural tractors, and military Mack artillery haulers.

Above: Yacht and boat transport were regular features of Pickfords operations, but they were by no means confined to the gentler roads of the Midlands and south. In 1954 the company was called upon to move the hull of the old pleasure steamer *Countess of Bredalbane* from Loch Awe to Inverary along some of the most demanding hill roads on Scotland's west coast. Once again it was a job for the veterans, and as so often was the case during the postwar years, there was an R100 – its military origins only thinly disguised beneath a ballast body – to take the strain.

Below: When the veterans were eventually replaced, Constructor proved to be a worthy successor. Work for the ballast-bodied versions of the heavy tractor frequently verged on the spectacular – as for example when Pickfords were awarded the contract to move the 79ton ex-GWR locomotive *Caerphilly Castle* and its 25ton tender to London's Science Museum. The special transporter – which incorporated railway lines for ease of loading – measured 42ft in length and together with the locomotive tipped the scales at nearly 100 tons. Two Constructors in tandem provided the traction for the 90ft 'road train', and the tender was moved by a third on a similar trailer.

Above: Throughout the 1960s loads got larger. At the time that this photograph was taken, the yacht *Manito* seen en route from Port Hamble to Southampton was the largest keeled yacht ever to have been moved by road in the UK. Although the weight was relatively light by Pickfords' standards, its dimensions were such that some delicate handling was necessary. The tractor was a 6×4 Constructor.

Below: Superlatives are liberally scattered throughout the annals of the heavy haulage industry, but even routine deliveries are not without complication. A Constructor negotiating the streets of Lincoln as a Ruston diesel locomotive sets out on the first leg of its journey to Portugal.

Below: Heavy haulage versions of Constructor were also taken into service by civil engineering specialists both to haul their increasingly bulky items of plant to and from construction sites, and to carry major prefabricated structural components. Marples Ridgway & Partners used one of its fleet in conjunction with a 20ton low loader trailer to transport the prestressed beams required for the construction of elevated roadworks at London's Hammersmith flyover.

Right: By the time that Contractor made its 1965 debut, new concepts in transportation were beginning to transform road haulage from a nationally-based industry into one in which international transits and interworking between hauliers of differing nationalities were the accepted practice. Not the least of these was the Roll on-Roll of ferry which enabled British and continental hauliers to devise factory-to-customer services as a viable alternative to the traditional multi-stage transit. The subsequent spectacular growth in such through routings was not confined to general hauliers, and several major ferry operators introduced facilities for the shipment of outsize trailer-borne loads. A 240ton (243 tonnes) GTW combination comprising a 1967 Contractor powered by a 450bhp Cummins diesel coupled to a Crane Fruehauf low-bed trailer 'rolls off' the ferry *Tor Anglia* at Immingham carrying an 85ton Roll-Housing in transit from Amsterdam to Sheffield.

Below right: As a 150ton heavy haulage tractor for semi-trailers, Contractor had a wheelbase of 4.70m and despite its capacity, a turning circle of only 24m. The 12.806tonne tractor was powered by a Cummins NTC355 diesel engine as were the military tank transporter, 85, 100, 120, and 180 ton versions. The Wynn's 150ton tractor shown here is at the head of a 130ton combination at Pandoro's Fleetwood ferry terminal. The load – one of the largest to be disembarked at the Northern Irish port of Larne – was an 85ton Crossley Pielstick marine diesel destined for Harland & Woolf's Belfast shipyard.

Above: Pulling Power. With two Contractors hauling, and a third pushing at the rear of the massive trailer, a 270ton transformer by Bruce Peebles Ltd of Edinburgh negotiates a steep gradient as it nears the South of Scotland Electricity Board's Longannet generating station.

Below: Crusader's versatility ensured it a place in many heavy transport operators' fleets. The 100ton CR100 version possesssed driveline and 'on the road' characteristics that fitted it for a variety of tasks ranging from hauling earthmoving plant to the carriage of 'one-off' modules of refinery equipment, and its future was thus assured at a time when many manufacturers were heavily committed to the production of fabrications for the North Sea and Middle Eastern oilfields. A Wynn's Crusader checks in to the Container Terminal at Bristol's Royal Portbury Dock with a typical 1980s'-style 'out of profile' item for shipment to the Middle East.

9 Postwar Military Vehicles

By the late 1940s Scammell could justifiably lay claim to status as a major force in the military vehicle sector of the truck market. However there could be no doubting that this reputation owed much to the Gardner powered R100s and recovery tractors which continued to soldier on not only with the British Army, but also with the forces of numerous allies, including those of Belgium, Denmark, and the Netherlands. Neither type could be expected to hold its place indefinitely in postwar inventories, and as Whitehall set about defining its requirements for the new standardised 'combat' and commercial-derived 'General Service' ranges of vehicle, a new recovery tractor was under development at Tolpits Lane.

The Explorer which began its service with the British Army in 1950 was a recovery unit in the GS category (ie not a combat vehicle) designed to retrieve disabled wheeled vehicles and armoured cars of up to 10ton in weight away from the battlefield. Like all GS vehicles it had to have the ability to climb a steep landing craft ramp,

and was fitted with switch-in all wheel drive engaged by a hand lever attached to the change gate. In many respects however Explorer was no more than an up-dated SV2/R100 with which it shared the familiar centrally-pivoted transverse spring front suspension layout. The 24in of wheel deflection that this layout permitted made Explorer a formidable vehicle away from prepared surfaces, but the turn of speed derived from a driveline comprising a six-cylinder Meadows petrol engine, six-speed constant mesh gearbox, and a centrally driven walking beam rear bogie, came as something of a surprise to those accustomed to the 'plodding' characteristics of the wartime-produced diesels.

The specification for the 26,180lb Explorer spoke demurely of a 29mph 'average' maximum speed, but belied the real potential of its 10,350cc, 185bhp engine, and at least one recovery team owed its escape from a terrorist ambush to Explorer's ability to accelerate rapidly to around twice its quoted maximum.

Above and top right: Without its bodywork, Explorer presented an impressive sight, and amply displayed the features that made it such a potent performer. Its 11ft 6in wheelbase was 8in shorter than that of its World War 2 ancestor, but although its unladen weight (26,180lb) was more than 2 tonne heavier it had a power to weight ratio of 13.9bhp per ton – considerably higher than those of most of its contemporaries.

Above: Explorer's recovery equipment comprised a 15.24tonne (15ton) main winch and a 4.57tonne (4.5ton) power-operated jib winch. A substantial order from the British Army – to whom it was known as FV11301 Tractor 10ton 6×6 GS Recovery – was followed by others from Egypt, New Zealand, and the Royal Air Force, who replaced Explorer's recovery equipment with a ballast box body and used it as a tractor for heavy drawbar trailers. The four vehicles supplied to New Zealand in 1959 were 'late' models which incorporated the cab and bonnet from the by then well-established FV1200 series of 20ton tractors developed by the British Army from the Constructor 6×6. The New Zealand vehicles were fitted with Meadows diesel engines in place of the customary IC unit from the same manufacturer. Like several of its predecessors, Explorer could also be fitted with a chain 'track' to improve its performance in marginal conditions.

Above: Inevitably the 4×4 Mountaineer's performance in tough overseas environments had attracted the attention of the British services, whose inventory at that time included no modern tractor unit capable of hauling engineer plant over the unprepared country in which they might be called upon to operate. Their requirement when eventually framed called for a six-wheeler derived from a commercial type with both ballast body, and the capability to be adapted as a tractor for semi-trailers. The early 1950s therefore saw Scammell simultaneously developing Constructor for both civilian and military markets. The basic ballasted tractor was initially produced for the British Army as FV12101 with the 15.24 tonne winch, wooden ballast body, and six-cylinder Meadows 6PC630 petrol engine as fitted to Explorer but later models were fitted with a partitioned steel body and a small davit for handling heavy equipment.

Below: FV12102 was the British Army version of Constructor as a winch-equipped tractor for 30.5 tonnes Engineer Plant semi-trailers. By the 1960s, the appearance of the military vehicle reflected the progressive improvements that Scammell had made to Constructor since its debut a decade previously. The cycle-type wings – and in some cases bar-type front fenders had been replaced by others of more substantial design, the exhaust had been re-routed through a vertical stack, and an array of stowage lockers added. There were less obvious changes too. The rear track was significantly narrower, and the roof-line lower, but since its introduction the tractor's weight had increased by 1.25 tonnes, and in terms of power to weight ratio military Constructors were losing the advantage that they had once enjoyed over their contemporaries. Unlike the tractor for full trailer version, FV12102 was fitted with a Rolls-Royce C6NFL six-cylinder in-line diesel developing 184bhp at 2,100rpm.

Below: The third military version of Constructor to be purchased in quantity by the UK Ministry of Defence was FV12105 a tractor for full trailer, 20 of which were purchased by the Royal Air Force from 1960 onwards. Like FV12102, to which it was mechanically similar, this 6×6 general cargo truck was still 'on offer' by Scammell in the early 1970s despite the fact that it no longer had domestic orders outstanding. As a cargo carrier FV12105 could operate at a maximum gross weight of 26.9tonne, although in the tractor role it was usually used in conjunction with the 30.5tonne trailer.

Bottom: Although Contractor did not enter general service with the British Army, the 6×4 tank transporter was purchased by several armies in the Middle East and Africa. Vehicles supplied to the Jordanian Army in 1971 were equipped with cab air-conditioning, and were capable of hauling a 61tonne tank at speeds of up to 46mph over ranges of around 300 miles. Contractor's 335bhp Cummins diesel drove via the 15 speeds of a Fuller RTO 12515 range change gearbox and a heavy duty 40.6tonne tandem bogie rear axle.

Above: As a maximum weight tank transporter, Contractor was usually paired with a matched Crane Fruehauf 61tonne low-bed semi-trailer. However Contractor's desert pedigree also fitted for off-highway tasks at less than its maximum capability. This Jordanian Army vehicle is hauling two 11tonne US-built M113 armoured personnel carriers on a Dyson 30ton multi-purpose semi-trailer specifically designed for operation in Middle Eastern conditions. Optional equipment available with the Contractor tank transporter included cab sun canopy, winches of up to 36.3tonne capacity, ballast box body, and roof-mounted searchlights.

Below: In the 1970s, the British Army selected the 6×4 version of the Crusader tractor as its standard heavy equipment transporter for plant and equipment of up to 34.4tonnes weight. Operating in a 61tonne GCW mode, Crusader was fitted with a 305bhp Rolls-Royce Eagle diesel, and fuller 915 15speed gearbox. The total of 300 Crusaders purchased included a number of 38tonne GCW tractors for use by the Royal Corps of Transport as high-speed long haulers, and all were fitted with sleeper cabs. The vehicle shown here is being operated by the Royal Engineers to transport a 17tonne combat engineer tractor.

Below: Scammell resumed what many people regarded as its rightful place as supplier of recovery vehicles to the UK Armed Forces with the receipt of a 1976 order for 130 Crusader 6×4s fitted with Swedish-built EKA recovery gear. The British Army had some years previously made a limited purchase of some Volvo F88B tractors fitted with the EKA lift boom system, the lifting device of which centres around a main lift boom raised by a telescopic ram. A folding boom stems from the main boom, and houses a hydraulically operated extension used for reaching under disabled vehicles. The EKA D2030 system fitted to the Crusader was of modular design incorporating earth-spade type anchor legs, and front and main winches. The entire unit including accessories and stowage compartments weighed only 5.8 tonnes.

Left: In its recovery version, Crusader was fitted with the same six-cylinder Rolls-Royce Eagle as the heavy equipment transporter, and had a wheelbase of 4.75m compared with the 3.96m of the standard tractor unit. The cab provided accommodation for the driver and three crew members. Scammell has long been registered as complying in its manufacturing, component supply, service, finance, and quality control systems with Ministry of Defence Standard 05-21, and the exacting standards entailed apply to all products of the Tolpits Lane Works.

Above: A Crusader-EKA recovery unit uses its boom to lift an Alvis Stalwart high mobility load carrier onto suspended tow. The advantage claimed for the EKA system is that it is sufficiently versatile to meet the demands of increasingly heavy goods vehicles, and combines the flexibility of a winch-equipped vehicle with the lifting power of a fixed crane. As a military recovery vehicle, Crusader was required to be able to reach stranded vehicles operating well away from made-up roads.

Below: Crusader was also ordered by the UK Ministry of Defence as a 100ton GCW heavy haulage tractor for use in situations where a military type would be either too conspicuous, or politically inappropriate. For the heavy haulage role the 6×4 could be supplied with engines and transmission components that were compatible with Contractors.

Above: The 6×4 Rolls-Royce engined Commander first shown to the public at the 1978 Motor Show as the probable replacement for the British Army's ageing fleet of Antar tank transporters from the mid-1980s, was of necessity one of the most impressive vehicles ever to emerge from Tolpits Lane. With combat weights of heavily armoured main battle tanks exceeding 60 tonnes, Commander was required to have a gross train weight of 104 tonnes, yet be capable of climbing a 1 in 40 gradient at 22mph when fully laden, and of attaining 39mph on level roads. Unlike the M911 tank transporter adopted by the US Army, which was an 'off the peg' civilian heavy hauler adapted to a military role, Commander was built primarily as a tank transporter with the possibility of additional sales to civilian customers as something of a bonus – nevertheless it was a considerably less complex piece of machinery than some of its highly specialised all wheel drive NATO contemporaries.

Commander's power unit was a V-12 Rolls-Royce CV 12TCE turbocharged diesel with water-cooled air charge rated at 625bhp at 2,100rpm, and with maximum torque of 1680lbf ft at 1,400rpm, but a 600bhp Cummins KTA 600 was available as an alternative. Drive was via a semi-automatic Allison CLBT 6061 transmission system incorporating a six-speed epicyclic gearbox, torque converter, and an integral retarder fitted to supplement the braking system on down-grades.

The four-man steel cab was based on the familiar Motor Panels Mk IV module arranged for left-hand drive and fitted with two sleeper berths. Particular attention was devoted to the provision of a high standard of crew comfort on long hauls, and the entire vehicle was engineered for ease of maintenance – there was a light glassfibre bonnet cover, and a layout that left sufficient space for a fitter to stand comfortably between the main frame members and the engine. Commander was fitted with a Turner 20.3tonne horizontal drum winch with 110m of 26mm cable for self-loading.

Some idea of Commander's capabilities may be gained from the fact that BAOR military trials team charged with the evaluation of the Rolls-engined prototype reported that one of it's biggest problems was the average German motorist's complete inability to correctly judge the speed of the tank transporter whenever it loomed ahead – years of contending with lumbering Antar-drawn outfits had left them quite unprepared for a 100ton combination with such performance.

Above: Commander undergoing user trials in the hands of the Royal Corps of Transport. The operational requirement for the British Army's tank transporter combination until the turn of the century calls for a laden height of less than four metres, and braking comparable with that of a 32tonne goods vehicle. Crane Fruehauf Developed a new Class 90 trailer specifiically for use in combination with the Scammell tractor. The 14.26tonne trailer seen in this photograph carrying a Chieftain tank, has an overall length of 13.17m and can be loaded with an immobilised tank by only two men using Commander's 25ton winch. Two Commanders were retained in the UK for trials purposes from 1978 onwards, and a third was shipped to Iran where it remained until the 1979 revolution brought plans for joint Anglo-Iranian development of the vehicle to a premature end.

Below: 1980 saw the debut of a new Explorer, a recovery vehicle developed by Reynolds Boughton as a fit for the Super Constructor 6×6, but exhibited at that year's British Army Equipment Exhibition on a Contractor 6×6. The 10-tonnes heavy recovery slewing crane was mounted on a roller bearing ring, and could be rotated through 270deg by a hydraulic motor. All slewing, luffing to a maximum of 45deg and hoisting were controlled from a turret platform. A 10.610tonne Reynolds Boughton winch was mounted crossways behind the cab. This particular vehicle was the subject of a 'one-off' purchase by the British Army against a specialised requirement for an all-wheel drive slewing crane recovery tractor.

10 Crash Fire and Rescue

Scammell's move into the highly specialised crash, fire and rescue vehicle field was a logical development of the series of mergers which brought AEC into the Leyland camp.

AEC had itself earlier acquired with Thornycroft more than 30 years of experience with specialist airfield vehicles, but apart from taking on the responsibility for existing Nubian, and Nubian Major models, Scammell found itself confronted by an urgent need to re-engineer the range in order to comply with increasingly stringent legislation. In 1978 two new Nubians – a 4×4 and a 6×6 – were launched. Both were powered by developed versions of the Cummins V903 diesel driving through a five-speed Allison automatic transmission, and Kirkstall

auxiliary gearbox. A Scammell-designed power take-off catered for pumping at up to 1,900gal per minute, and there was a facility for pumping whilst the vehicle was on the move. Like their predecessors, the Nubians were supplied in chassis form with specialist constructors contributing fire-fighting and rescue equipment. There was accommodation for a three-man crew in a Motor Panels Mk IV cab which afforded the rapid entry and exit necessary in an airfield CFR vehicle. Cab layout followed current practice for high mobility vehicles with the driver being provided with a central seating position sufficiently far forward to permit him the maximum degree of control when travelling at high speeds off-highway.

Above: As the basis of a 4×4 crash tender with a gross weight of up to 18.29 tonnes, Nubian was available as either Nubian 2 powered by the 300bhp naturally aspirated V903, or the Super Nubian with a 400bhp turbocharged version of the same V-8 diesel. Optional 13.00-20 or 16.00-20 tyres made it possible to use the chassis as the basis of major rescue appliances or rapid intervention vehicles without compromising the low centre of gravity. In its maximum weight configuration, the Nubian 2 could

accelerate from a standing start to 50mph in 40 seconds, and the 6×6 to the same speed in only 31 seconds. The new Nubians were launched at a time when they and every opportunity to capitalise on Scammell's reputation in the Middle East to gain a share of that region's blooming economy, but they were also the subject of a vigorous sales campaign in the fiercely competitive United States market.

Top: Chubb Fire Vehicles was one of several manufacturers of approved firefighting equipment to market purpose-built vehicles on the Nubian chassis. The Chubb Protector 2 is built on the 4.75m wheelbase Nubian 6×6 using either the 400bhp VT903 engine, or the turbocharged and aftercooled VTA903 rated at 500bhp. Although UK legislation limited vehicles of Nubian's dimensions to a maximum on-highway weight of 24.38 tonnes, their design maximum of 28.45 tonnes meant that the 500bhp Super Major version had an off-highway water capacity of 11,365 litres (2,800gal).

The Chubb Protector equipment fit as illustrated in this 1978 vehicle built for use at Accra International Airport (Ghana) includes a monitor and pump module incorporating a Godiva Mk 14 pump, a midships locker module containing rescue equipment, hosereels, and handlines, and an up to 9, 100-litres tank module.

Quoted performance figures were 0-50mph in 44 seconds and 38 seconds respectively for the 400 and 500 bhp models.

Below left: Gloster Saro, another top hamper manufacturer selected the Nubian 4×4 as the basis for its Gladiator CFR vehicles, which it produced in a number of configurations between 14-18.3 tonnes. At the lower end of their weight range, Gladiator crash tenders had a performance approaching that of a rapid intervention vehicle, and like all Nubian-based vehicles could be manoeuvered at 5mph whilst delivering their maximum pump output. The main fire-fighting control and indicator panel was located at the front of the crew compartment, where the instrumentation also included contents gauges for up to 6,000 litres of tank capacity. Gladiator's extensive range of optional equipment included radio, underbody and groundsweep nozzles, and a lightweight GRP water tank.

Top right: A Chubb Protector 2 4×4 supplied to Bournemouth (Hurn) Airport in 1980. The standard foam system could deliver up to 1,800 litres each minute via a roof-mounted monitor capable of rotation through 264-degrees, 45-degrees elevation, and five degrees of depression. An optional system (which was the lower rated of the two systems available for the 6×6 version of Protector) could deliver 3,180 litres per minute at 14 bar pressure. The vehicle could be used on a 30-degree sideslope, and 18.3m kerb-to-kerb turning capability combined with 30-degree approach/departure angles and air-operated differential locks to make it highly manouverable when operating away from roads and prepared surfaces.

Right: The 1980 Chubb Protector 6×6 demonstrator incorporated a restyled cab. Scammell sold approximately 20 Nubian 2s during 1979, and at the end of that year had shipped a demonstration chassis cab to the United States where marketing surveys had revealed a sales potential for between 20 and 30 vehicles each year. The vehicle illustrated was constructed in response to a British Airports Authority requirement for a new generation of CFR equipment to cope with the risks entailed by increased volumes of traffic, and although it failed to gain acceptance it attracted considerable interest elsewhere.

11 Into the 1980s

The 1970s had brought many changes to Scammell. In 1972 Leyland had centralised the sales and marketing functions for its entire range of commercial vehicles, and although the Watford division retained its own assets and specialised design and development teams it lost its much-prized autonomy. The new role as the 'Scammell Motors Plant', a manufacturing unit of the Heavy Vehicles Division of Leyland Truck and Bus, was relatively short-lived, but unpopular as it was with Scammell people it is possible to see it as a necessary part of the process of 'clearing the decks' which eventually enabled Leyland Vehicles to enter the 1980s with a much slimmer product range and a more combative marketing strategy than had at one time seemed likely.

Leyland was in fact fighting for its survival, and there was much concern both at Scammell and amongst their customers that the absence of a specialist marketing arm was a disadvantage in those markets where it was the Scammell reputation rather than that of Leyland that sold trucks. There was therefore understandable relief at Tolpits Lane when in 1976 Leyland decided that there should be a further reorganisation which would enable the group to build upon its acknowledged strengths. Scammell emerged from the reshuffle with at least a measure of its former independence, a reconstituted marketing department, and a product range which had been trimmed to suit its new role as the Heavy Vehicle Division's Special Purpose and Military Vehicles subsidiary.

Crusader 4×2 had gone, but the 6×4 was still selling well particularly in export markets and would be retained until at least the early 1980s – a tribute to the expertise which made it such a seller in an increasingly competitive market place – but its replacement on the customary 4-5

years time scale was one of Scammell's top priorities as they 'came in from the cold'. In the meantime LVL's plans to produce an entirely new range of trucks with a high degree of component commonality were nearing fruition. Thus as Scammell built the prototype of the new Commander its designers were also deeply involved in the development of the new Leyland Landtrain range which was eventually launched in 1980 as the new generation of 19-30tonne bonneted prime movers for overseas markets (although some tractors were rated at up to 65tonne GCW).

The new range perpetuated the Scammell tradition of considerable overload design standard, and incorporated a chassis which was basically Contractor's, and a new bogie suspension unit derived from that fitted to the same vehicle.

Below: Leylands's policy for the 1980s – and therefore Scammell's too – was founded on the need to offer a rationalised range of products. The tipper seen here was very much a Scammell in design terms, but although LVL made particular capital of their subsidiary's contribution during the development phase, and of its experience with rugged off-highway vehicles, the name on the bonnet was Leyland.

Landtrain was followed into service by LVL's forward control Roadtrain 16.28, a maximum weight tractive unit for the UK only, and the spearhead of Leyland's fight back against the continental manufacturers who had made such inroads into the domestic market. Roadtrain was built to a premium specification, and incorporated a spacious all-steel cab which combined aerodynamic efficiency with a high standard of interior comfort, low noise levels, and exceptionally good visibility – precisely the cab which had been sought for the Routeman replacement.

Left: Routeman's successor, the Leyland Constructor which made its debut in mid-1980 incorporated the new cab, and a number of other refinements, but nevertheless provided a near classic demonstration of the merits of sticking to a winning formula. Like its immediate predecessor, the newcomer had a drive line comprising the Leyland T11 engine and six-speed constant mesh gearbox, with an optional 220bhp Rolls-Royce diesel, but there was also the opportunity for operators of the cargo version to specify Roadtrain's Spicer 10-speed 'splitter' box.

One significant point of difference underlined LVL's determination to rationalise. Prior to its launch, the new eight-wheeler had been generally spoken of at Watford as 'Routeman 4', and although it ultimately appeared with a name that did in fact perpetuate a Scammell tradition, the badge that it bore was that of the Leyland parent. It was a move that aroused considerable comment, until eventually LVL conceded the point and agreed to a smaller Scammell badge being placed alongside the Constructor name.

Above: As Leyland Vehicles' special purpose vehicles division, Scamell's responsibilities for the 1980s began at that point where those of the Landtrain team left off. A new range – known as the S24 series was developed as part of LVL's overall marketing strategy, and launched at the 1980 Birmingham Motor Show with the objective of establishing a strong group presence in the 50-300tonne heavy hauler category, based on the reputation of the Constructor/Super Constructor and Contractor series which it was to supersede, but conforming with the overall rationalisation plan.

The CT40 truck/tractor chassis – shown here as the basis of a mobile concrete mixer for on/off highway use – was rated at 44tonne GVW (on/off highway), but could be adapted for involving up to 300 tonnes GCW in restricted road use. The extent of the bodywork commonality with Landtrain is readily discernible, but the entire S24 range was powered by the 350 bhp Cummins NTE350 'big cam' turbocharged/aftercooled diesel, and its suitability for any specific task was determined by the choice of transmission and tyre size. All modules were built on a flitched open-channel ladder chassis, and Scammell's particular expertise in the design of vehicles for the fiercely-competitive Middle Eastern markets was evident in the cooling system which incorporated twin radiators with a combined surface area of 8,300sq cm.

95

Above: As a scow-bodied heavy-duty dump truck, the S24 provided LVL with a powerful voice in a market that had been considerably stimulated by the efforts of continental manufacturers to persuade construction contractors that it was possible to obtain reliable site-dumping capability without investing in the more expensive specialist vehicles developed for the mining and quarrying industries.

S24's standard suspension comprised a fully articulating two semi-elliptic eight-leaf spring layout at the rear, in which the axles (rated at between 32-38,000kg) were located by radius and Panhard rods. Front suspension was by semi-elliptic leaf springs, and off-highway performance was enhanced by the provision of inter-axle and cross-axle differential locks on the hub-reduction driven axles.

Below: When Scammell developed its first on/off highway truck, its sales executives were quick to realise that its rear-bogie was one of its most photogenic features. So it has been that down the years, Pioneer, Mountaineer, the Constructors, the heavy dumpers, the oilfield trucks, the loggers and the military tractors have always been photographed crossing off highway obstacles. It is therefore only appropriate that this book should close with a shot that typifies Scammell as it enters the 1980s. The look of the truck is the look of Leyland as it fights to regain its share of world markets – the manner in which it is surmounting the obstacles in its path is unmistakeably Scammell, and says it all about 60 years of accumulated experience.